SHAZAM!
POWER OF HOPE

STORY BY ALEX ROSS AND PAUL DINI
TEXT BY PAUL DINI · ART BY ALEX ROSS

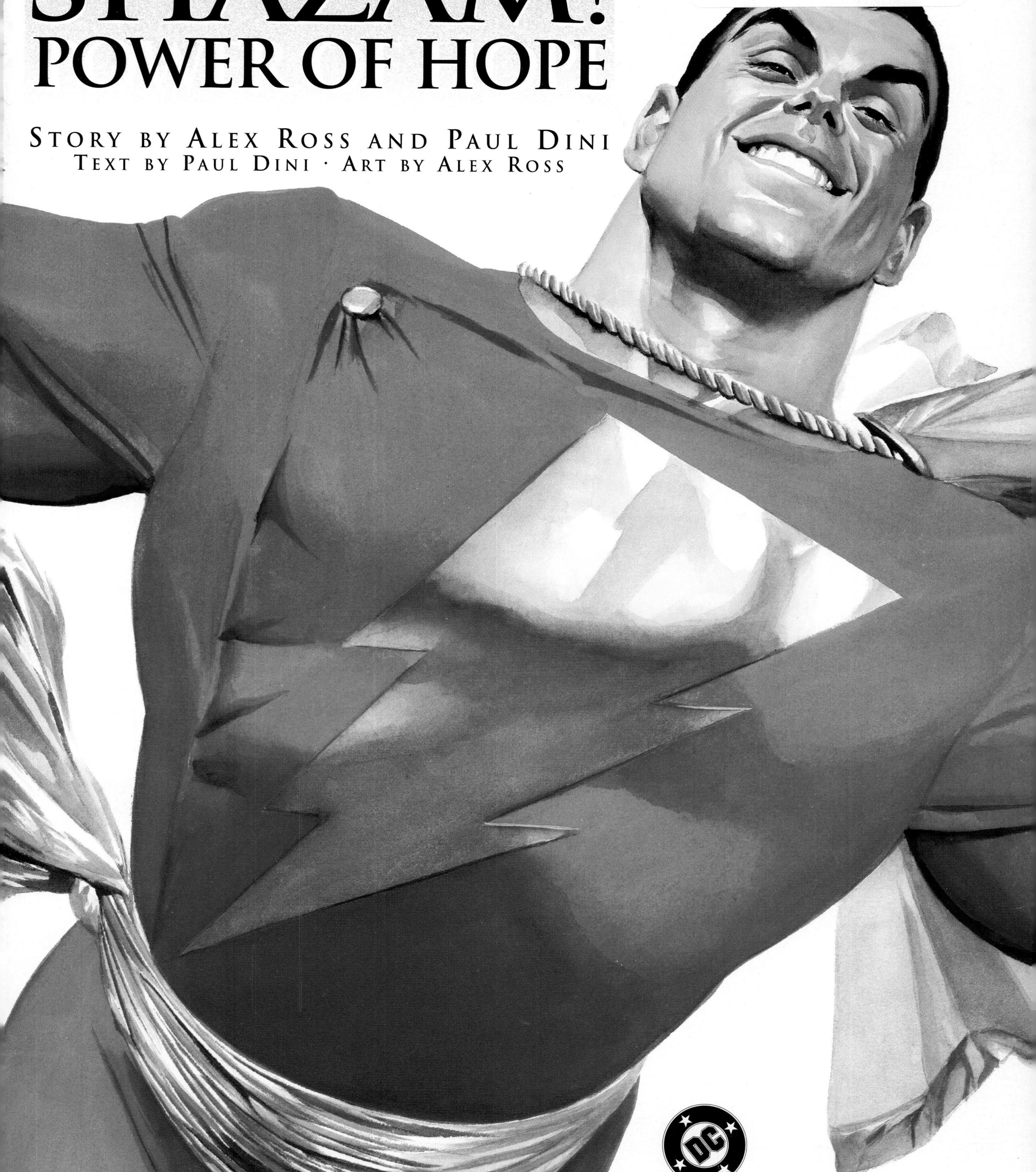

DC COMICS · NEW YORK

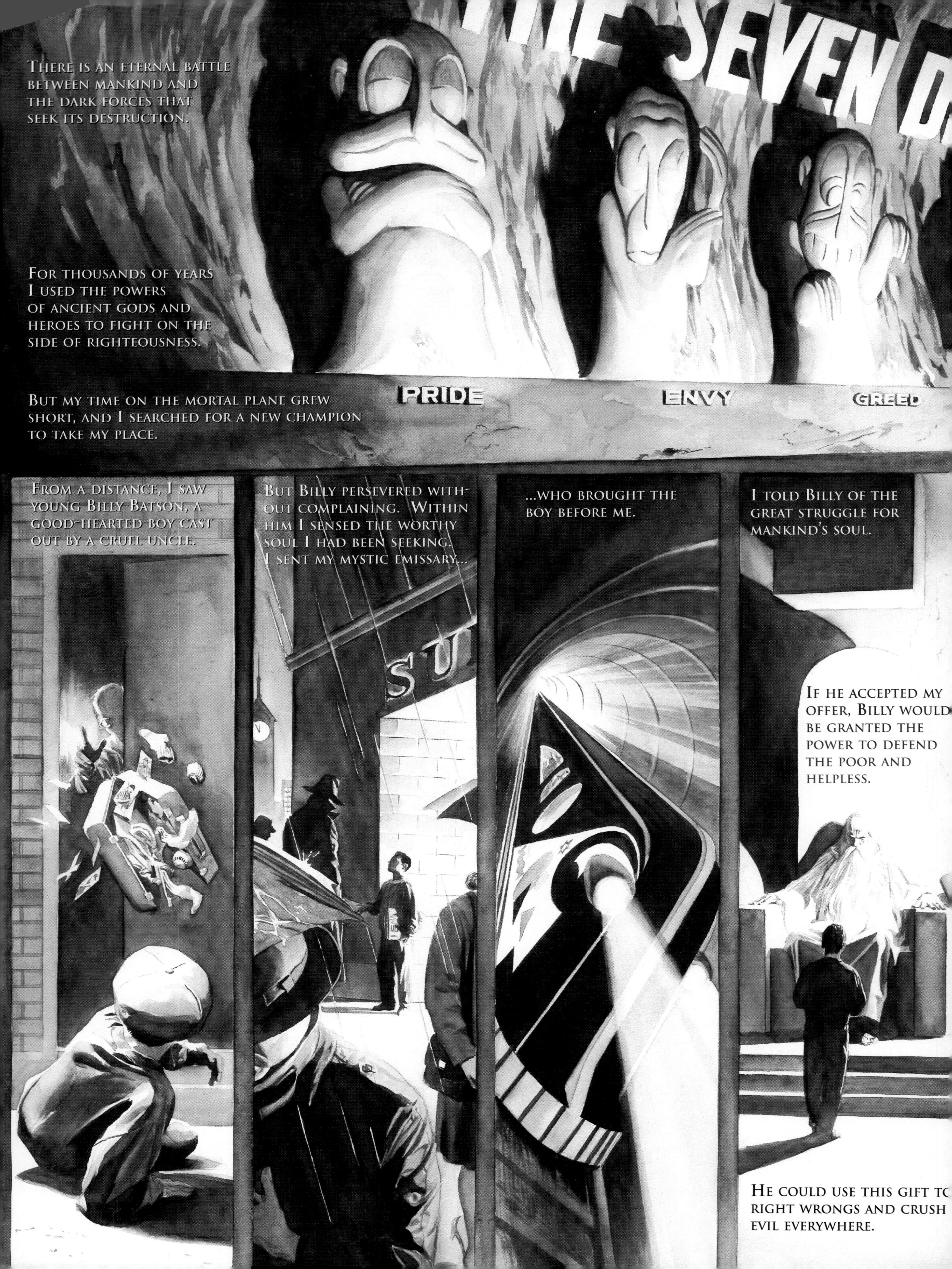
THE SEVEN D
There is an eternal battle between mankind and the dark forces that seek its destruction.
For thousands of years I used the powers of ancient gods and heroes to fight on the side of righteousness.
But my time on the mortal plane grew short, and I searched for a new champion to take my place.
PRIDE
ENVY
GREED
From a distance, I saw young Billy Batson, a good-hearted boy cast out by a cruel uncle.
But Billy persevered without complaining. Within him I sensed the worthy soul I had been seeking. I sent my mystic emissary...
SU
...who brought the boy before me.
I told Billy of the great struggle for mankind's soul.
If he accepted my offer, Billy would be granted the power to defend the poor and helpless.
He could use this gift to right wrongs and crush evil everywhere.

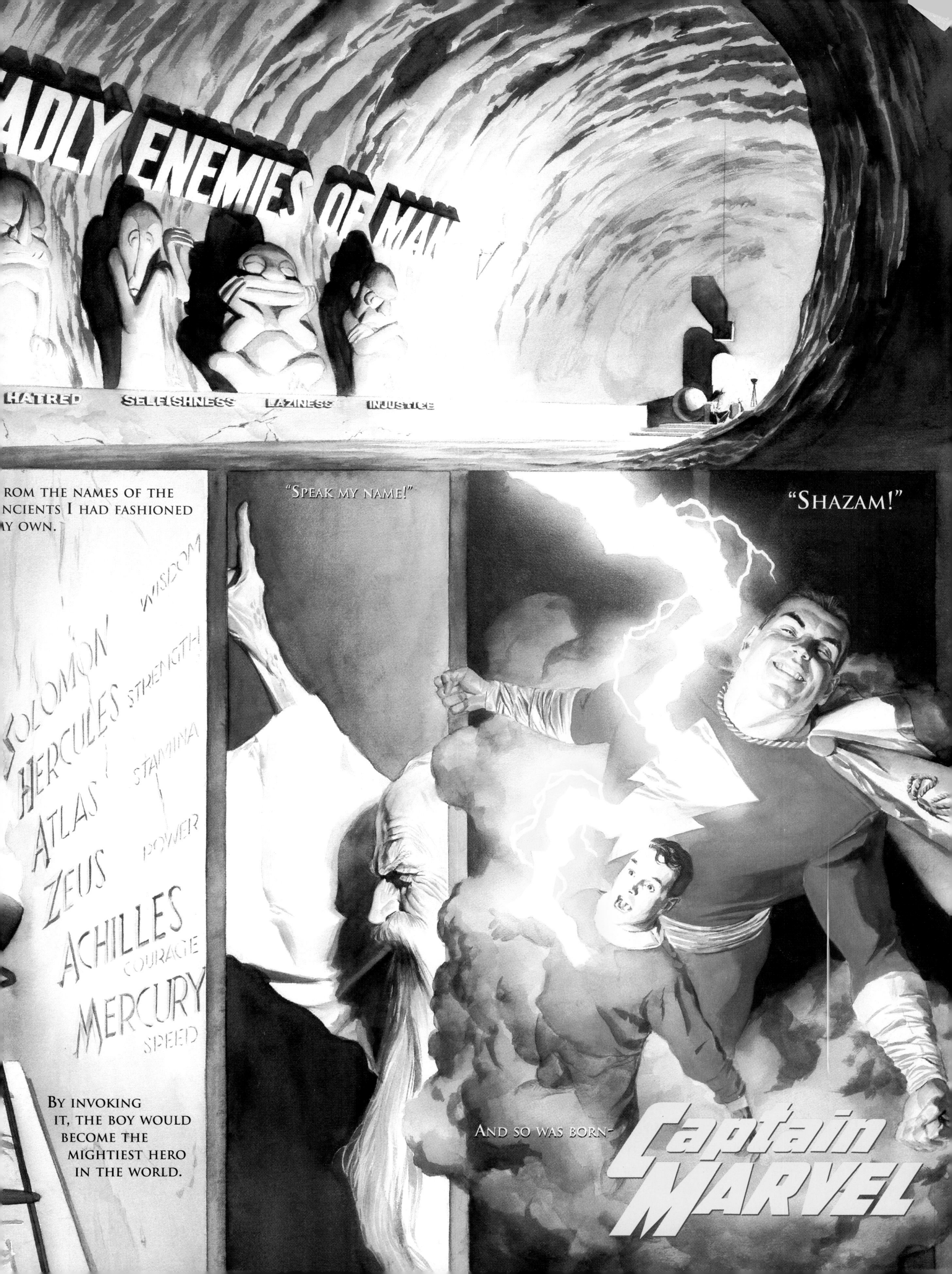

ADLY ENEMIES OF MAN
HATRED
SELFISHNESS
LAZINESS
INJUSTICE
ROM THE NAMES OF THE NCIENTS I HAD FASHIONED MY OWN.
SOLOMON WISDOM
HERCULES STRENGTH
ATLAS STAMINA
ZEUS POWER
ACHILLES COURAGE
MERCURY SPEED
BY INVOKING IT, THE BOY WOULD BECOME THE MIGHTIEST HERO IN THE WORLD.
"SPEAK MY NAME!"
"SHAZAM!"
AND SO WAS BORN–
Captain MARVEL

First, a deep bow of gratitude to a bunch of great kids, some relatives and some not, who each brighten my life simply by being in it. This one's for you, guys. Caitlin and Matt Dini, Alison and Emily McClaran, Hallie Jacobson, Katie Toles, Stephen and Jayna McClaran, Ford and Nell MacCarty, Christopher Dini, Claudia, Thomas, Megan, and Caroline Dini, Eli and Owen Lloyd, Annie, Kate, and Emmy Hamilton, Grace, Bobby, and Peter Brown, Allyson and Erica Langford, Mark Garabedian, Nathan, Luke and Cody Ruegger, Ryan Rogel, Cooper and Harper Sweeney, Samantha Timm, Christopher Whitfield Simmons, Harley Quinn Smith, Lauren and Connor McLaughlin, Rebecca and Andrew Fogel, and Nick, Melanie, and Andrea Burnett.

Next, a "100 Bullets" salute to Brian Azzarello for suggesting the touching final image of our story. Thanks for the great moment. Also thanks to Rob Simpson for the wonderful title.

The biggest thanks of all to the biggest kid of all, my dad, Bob Dini, who first told me stories of Billy Batson and Captain Marvel long before I ever read them in a comic book. The way he recounted Billy's first meeting with the old Wizard as well as the Captain's subsequent adventures filled me with a sense of wonder that no other versions of the characters (great as they are) have ever done. If any of that shows through in this text, that's his doing. Thanks, Dad.

—Paul Dini

For the fans of Captain Marvel, who keep the magic alive.

Sal Abbinanti, my long-suffering model for the Captain, is always a good sport to suffer the jibes of our friends who sling every "Big Red Cheese" epithet his way. This book really wouldn't have been worth doing without Sal, so if you see him at a convention, be nice. Thanks again to my dad, Clark Ross, for reprising his role as the Wizard Shazam.

Steve Duff, Darlene Hanna, and Laura Miller of the Rehabilitation Institute of Chicago provided much-needed exposure to a hospital environment and state-of-the-art treatments. For technical research, Tony Akins and Dave Riske were of great help. Teresa Vitale provided the wonderful costume I fashioned my work after.

The models who gave so freely of their time and patience are: T.J. Katz, Tyler and Cydney Duff, Mary Jo Rogers, Sung Koo, Logan and Mason Smith, Vlad, Eddie Gorodetsky, Coop, Ruth Waytz, Mark Ferreira, Tony Akins, Scott Beaderstadt, Steve Darnall, Gloria Chavez, and Tom Gianni.

Special gratitude to Zac Osgood for modeling as Bobby and for providing an entrance at Children's Memorial Hospital in Chicago, where Zac had built me up as a big shot to get a fantastic tour and photo reference. Beth Carona and Kathryn Carrico of the Children's Memorial Foundation treated me as an honored guest and gave me the best treatment I've received in trying to do research for this book series. Thanks also to Luis Duarte and Mark Byrd of the hospital's security for guiding us through this exceptional facility.

—Alex Ross

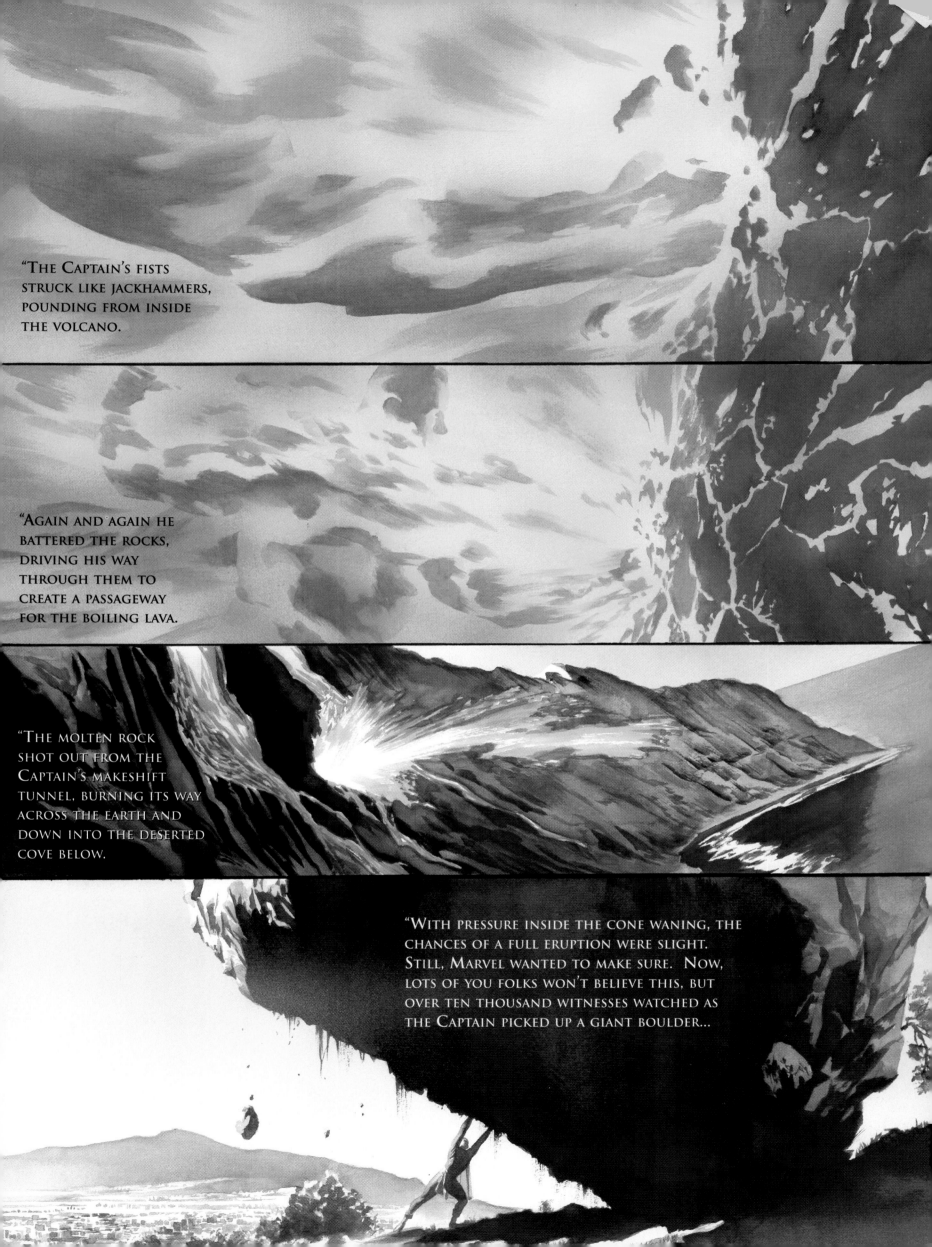

"THE CAPTAIN'S FISTS STRUCK LIKE JACKHAMMERS, POUNDING FROM INSIDE THE VOLCANO.

"AGAIN AND AGAIN HE BATTERED THE ROCKS, DRIVING HIS WAY THROUGH THEM TO CREATE A PASSAGEWAY FOR THE BOILING LAVA.

"THE MOLTEN ROCK SHOT OUT FROM THE CAPTAIN'S MAKESHIFT TUNNEL, BURNING ITS WAY ACROSS THE EARTH AND DOWN INTO THE DESERTED COVE BELOW.

"WITH PRESSURE INSIDE THE CONE WANING, THE CHANCES OF A FULL ERUPTION WERE SLIGHT. STILL, MARVEL WANTED TO MAKE SURE. NOW, LOTS OF YOU FOLKS WON'T BELIEVE THIS, BUT OVER TEN THOUSAND WITNESSES WATCHED AS THE CAPTAIN PICKED UP A GIANT BOULDER...

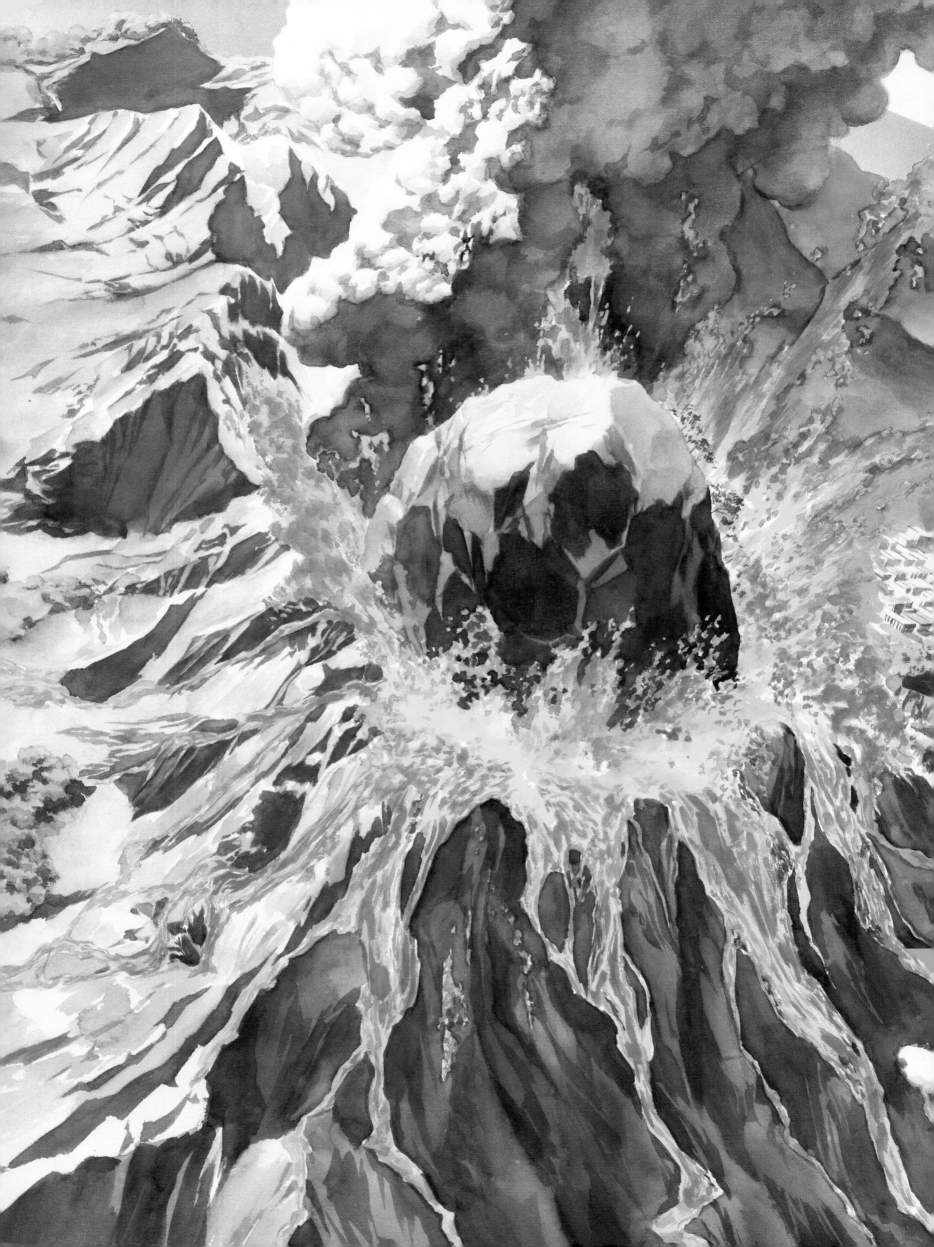

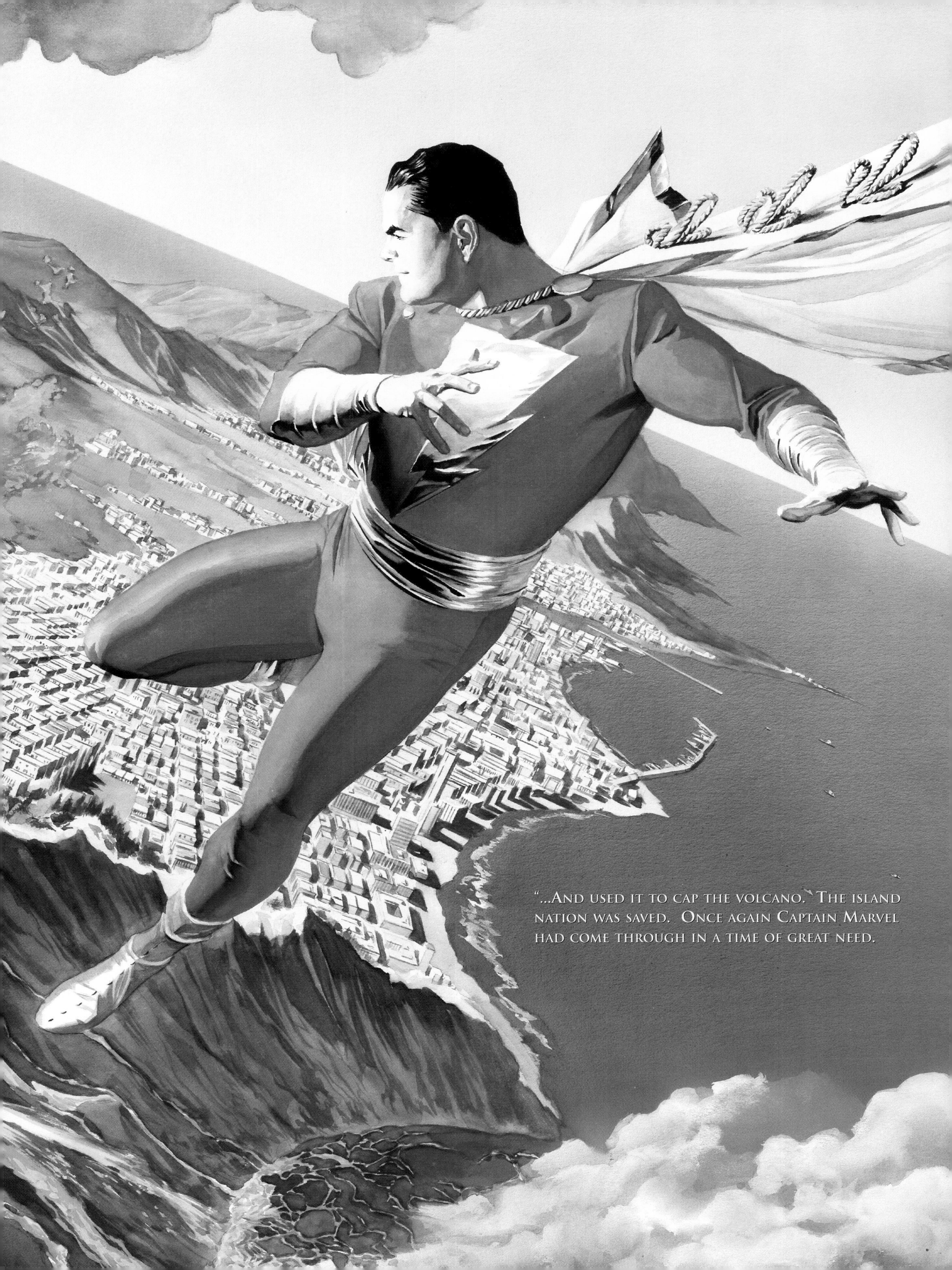
“...And used it to cap the volcano. The island nation was saved. Once again Captain Marvel had come through in a time of great need.

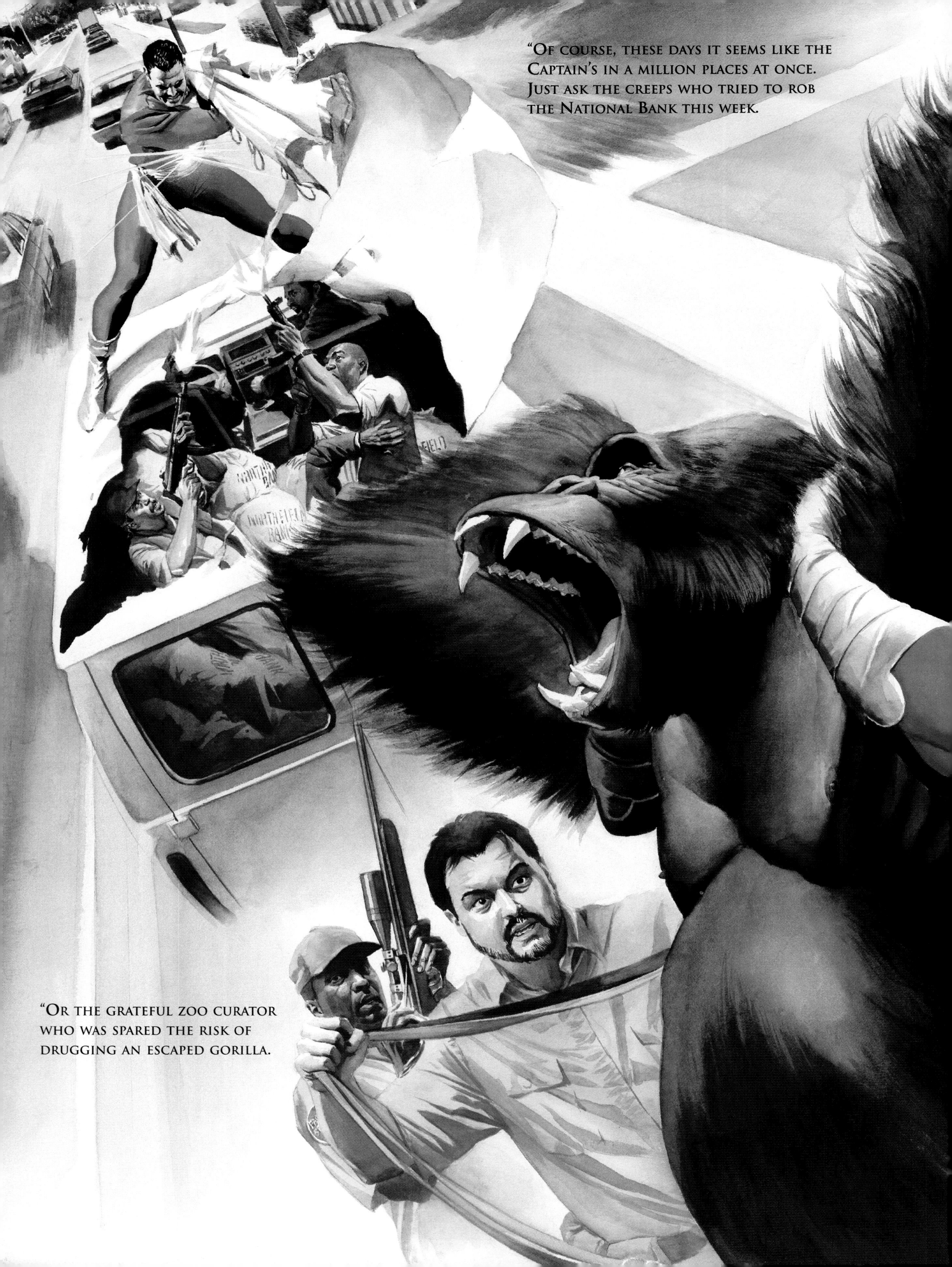
"Of course, these days it seems like the Captain's in a million places at once. Just ask the creeps who tried to rob the National Bank this week.
"Or the grateful zoo curator who was spared the risk of drugging an escaped gorilla.

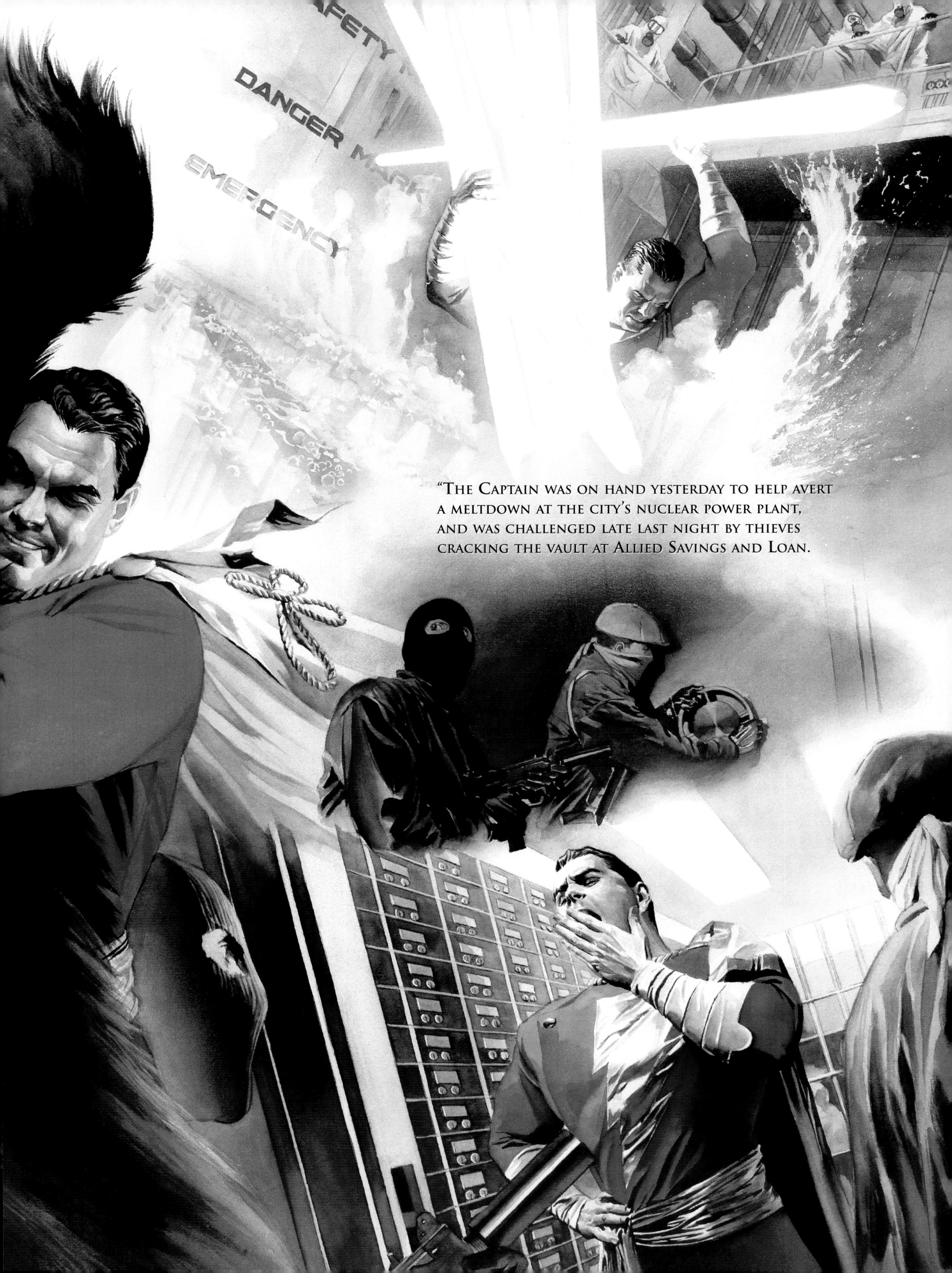
DANGER
EMERGENCY
“The Captain was on hand yesterday to help avert a meltdown at the city’s nuclear power plant, and was challenged late last night by thieves cracking the vault at Allied Savings and Loan.

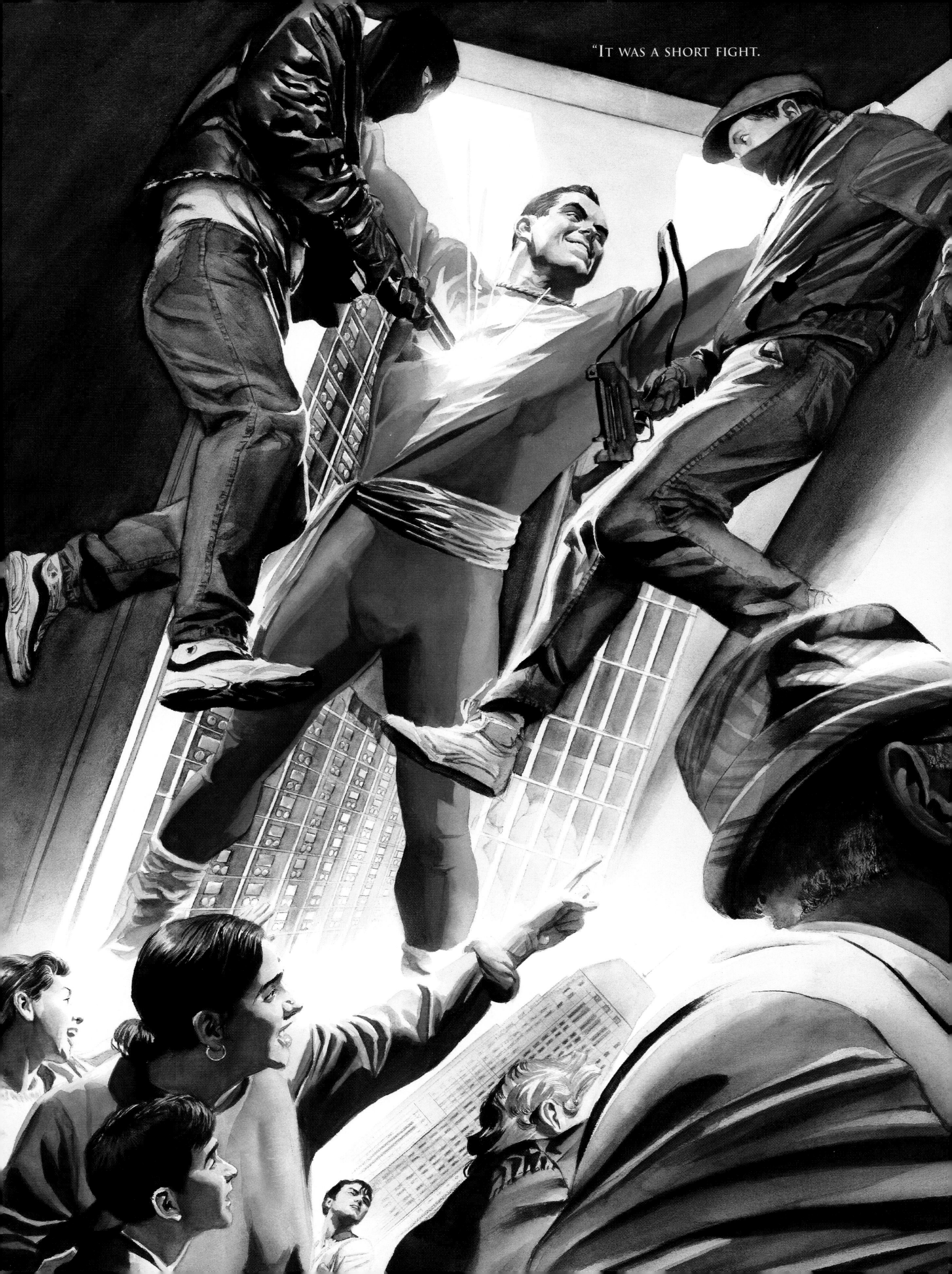
"It was a short fight.

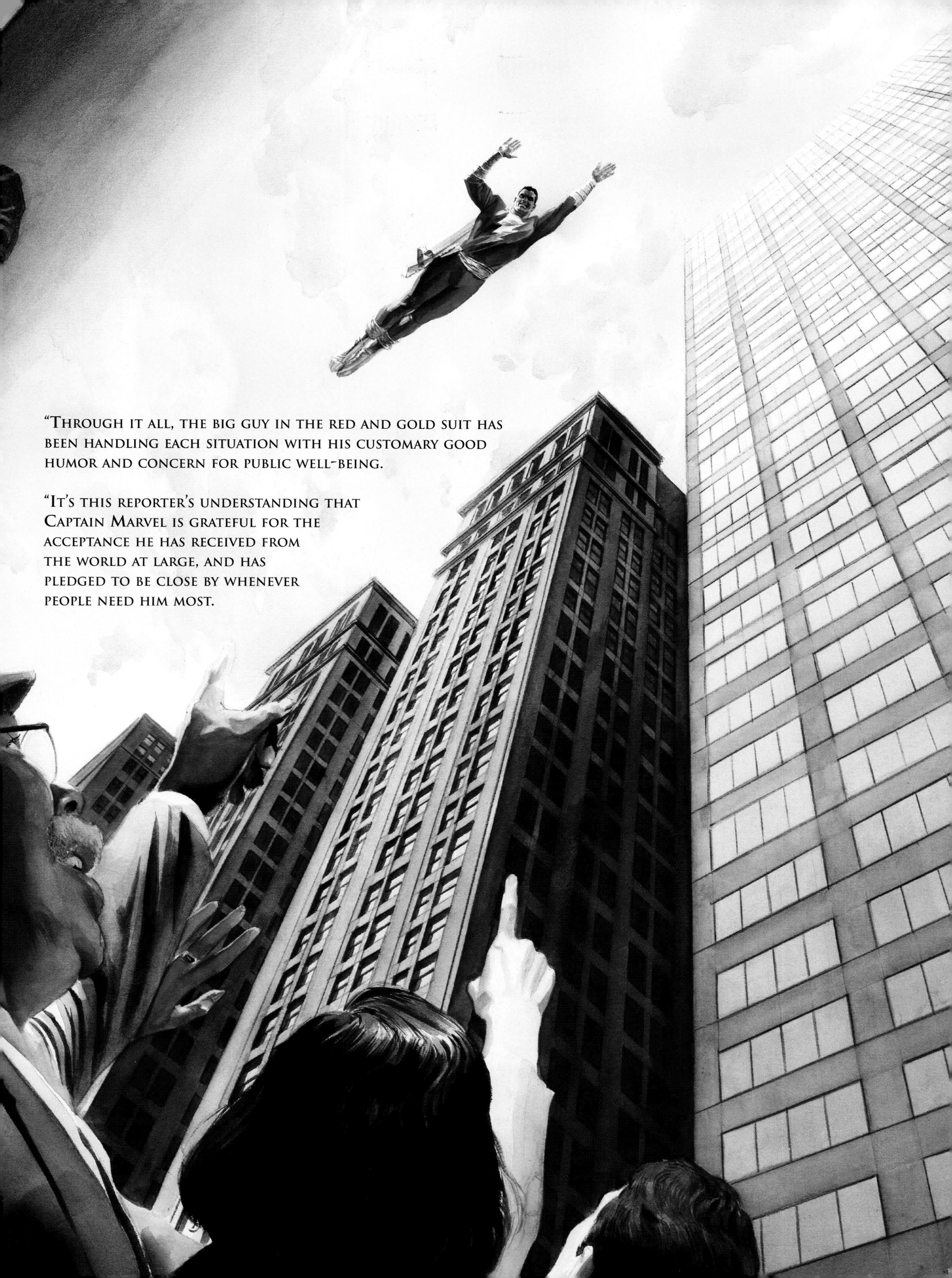
"Through it all, the big guy in the red and gold suit has been handling each situation with his customary good humor and concern for public well-being.
"It's this reporter's understanding that Captain Marvel is grateful for the acceptance he has received from the world at large, and has pledged to be close by whenever people need him most.

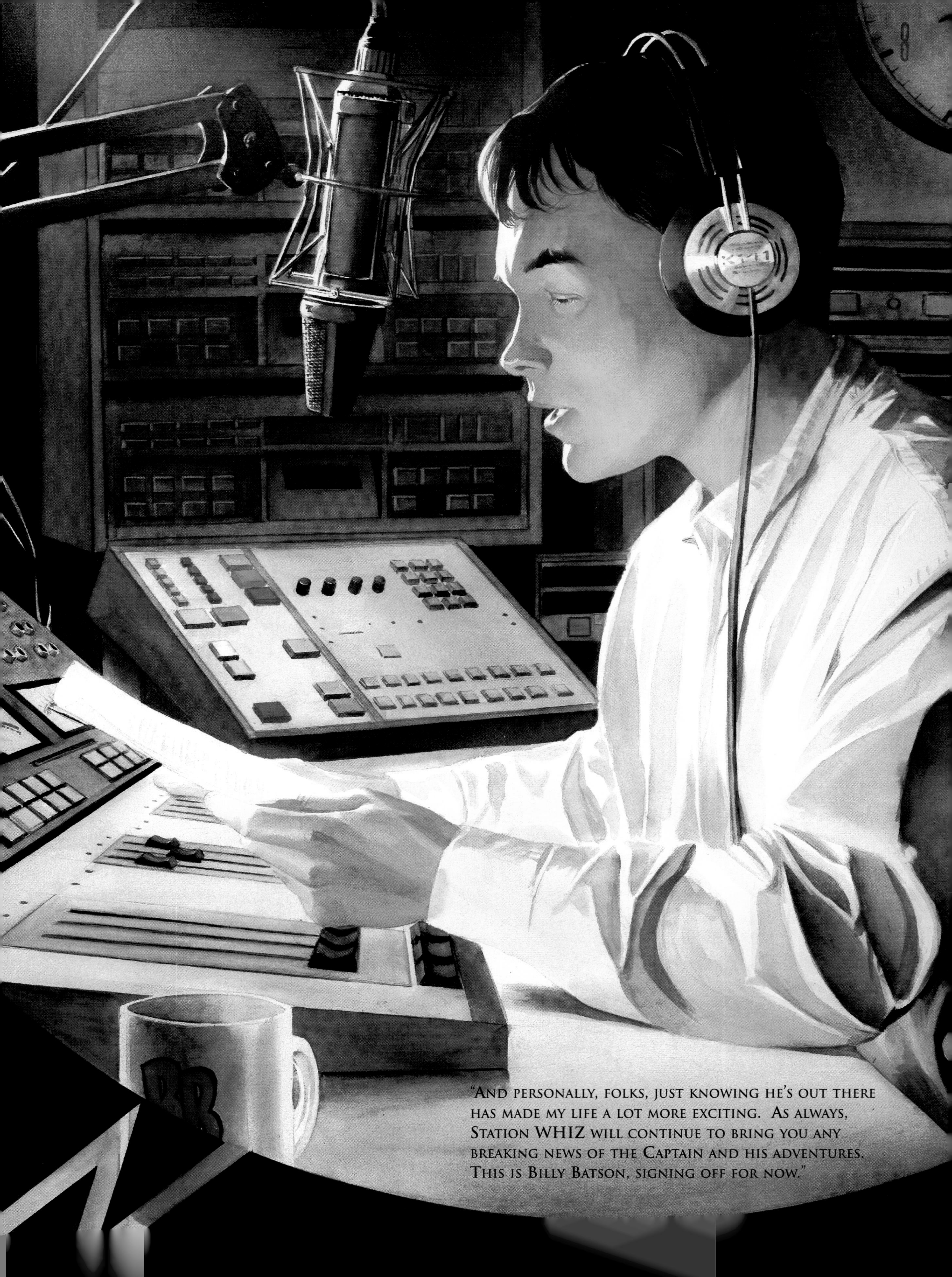
"And personally, folks, just knowing he's out there has made my life a lot more exciting. As always, Station WHIZ will continue to bring you any breaking news of the Captain and his adventures. This is Billy Batson, signing off for now."

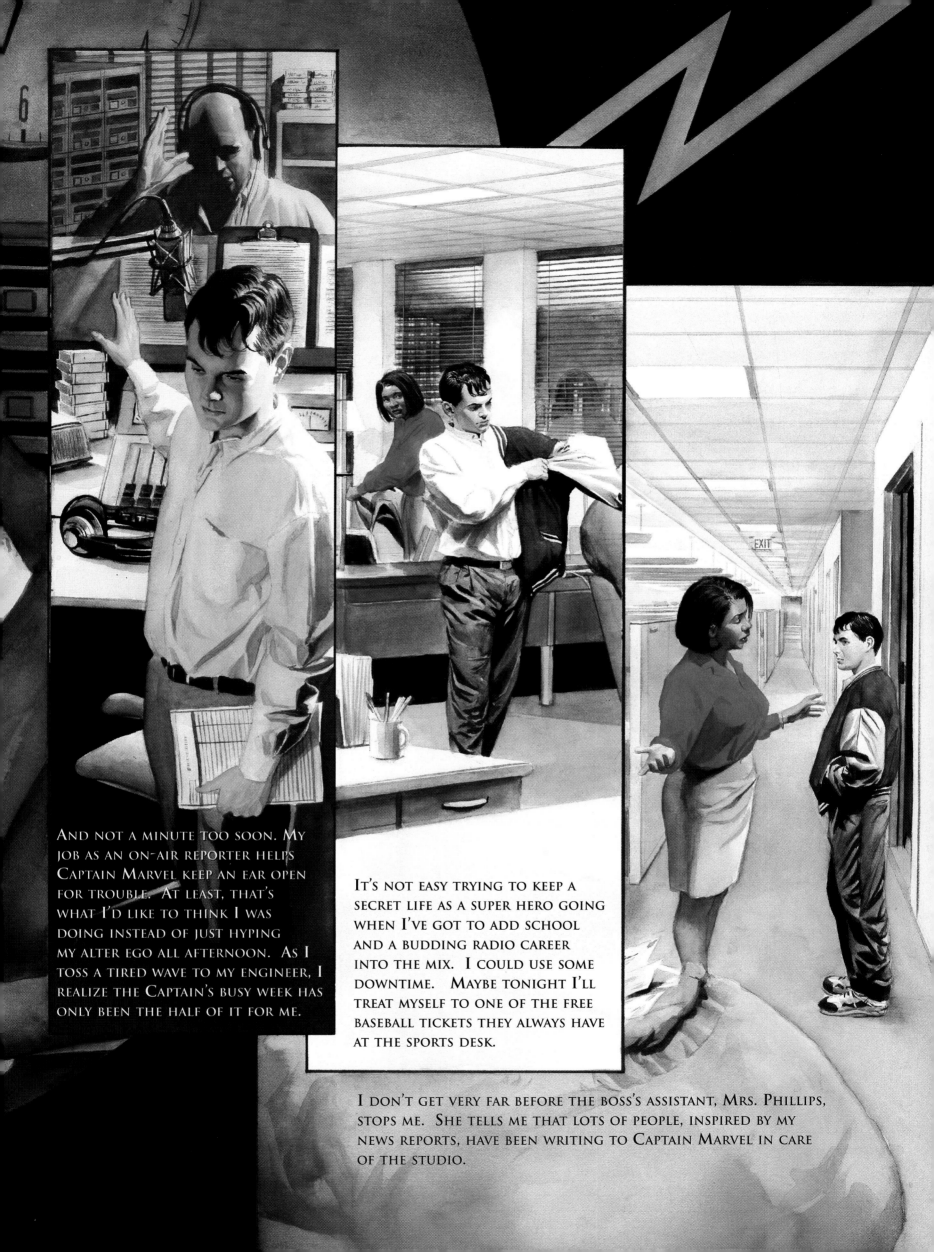

AND NOT A MINUTE TOO SOON. MY JOB AS AN ON-AIR REPORTER HELPS CAPTAIN MARVEL KEEP AN EAR OPEN FOR TROUBLE. AT LEAST, THAT'S WHAT I'D LIKE TO THINK I WAS DOING INSTEAD OF JUST HYPING MY ALTER EGO ALL AFTERNOON. AS I TOSS A TIRED WAVE TO MY ENGINEER, I REALIZE THE CAPTAIN'S BUSY WEEK HAS ONLY BEEN THE HALF OF IT FOR ME.

IT'S NOT EASY TRYING TO KEEP A SECRET LIFE AS A SUPER HERO GOING WHEN I'VE GOT TO ADD SCHOOL AND A BUDDING RADIO CAREER INTO THE MIX. I COULD USE SOME DOWNTIME. MAYBE TONIGHT I'LL TREAT MYSELF TO ONE OF THE FREE BASEBALL TICKETS THEY ALWAYS HAVE AT THE SPORTS DESK.

I DON'T GET VERY FAR BEFORE THE BOSS'S ASSISTANT, MRS. PHILLIPS, STOPS ME. SHE TELLS ME THAT LOTS OF PEOPLE, INSPIRED BY MY NEWS REPORTS, HAVE BEEN WRITING TO CAPTAIN MARVEL IN CARE OF THE STUDIO.

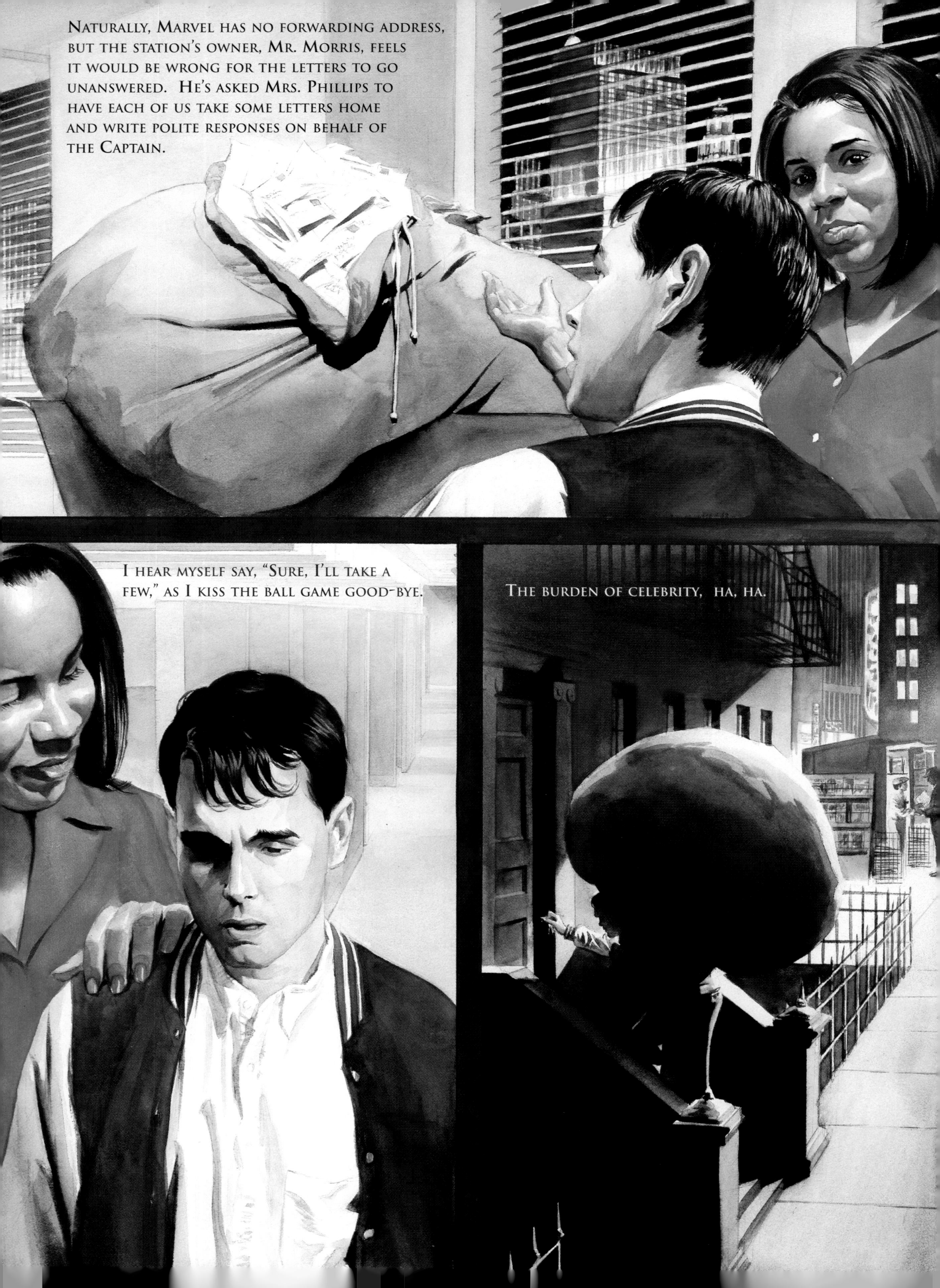
Naturally, Marvel has no forwarding address, but the station's owner, Mr. Morris, feels it would be wrong for the letters to go unanswered. He's asked Mrs. Phillips to have each of us take some letters home and write polite responses on behalf of the Captain.
I hear myself say, "Sure, I'll take a few," as I kiss the ball game good-bye.
The burden of celebrity, ha, ha.

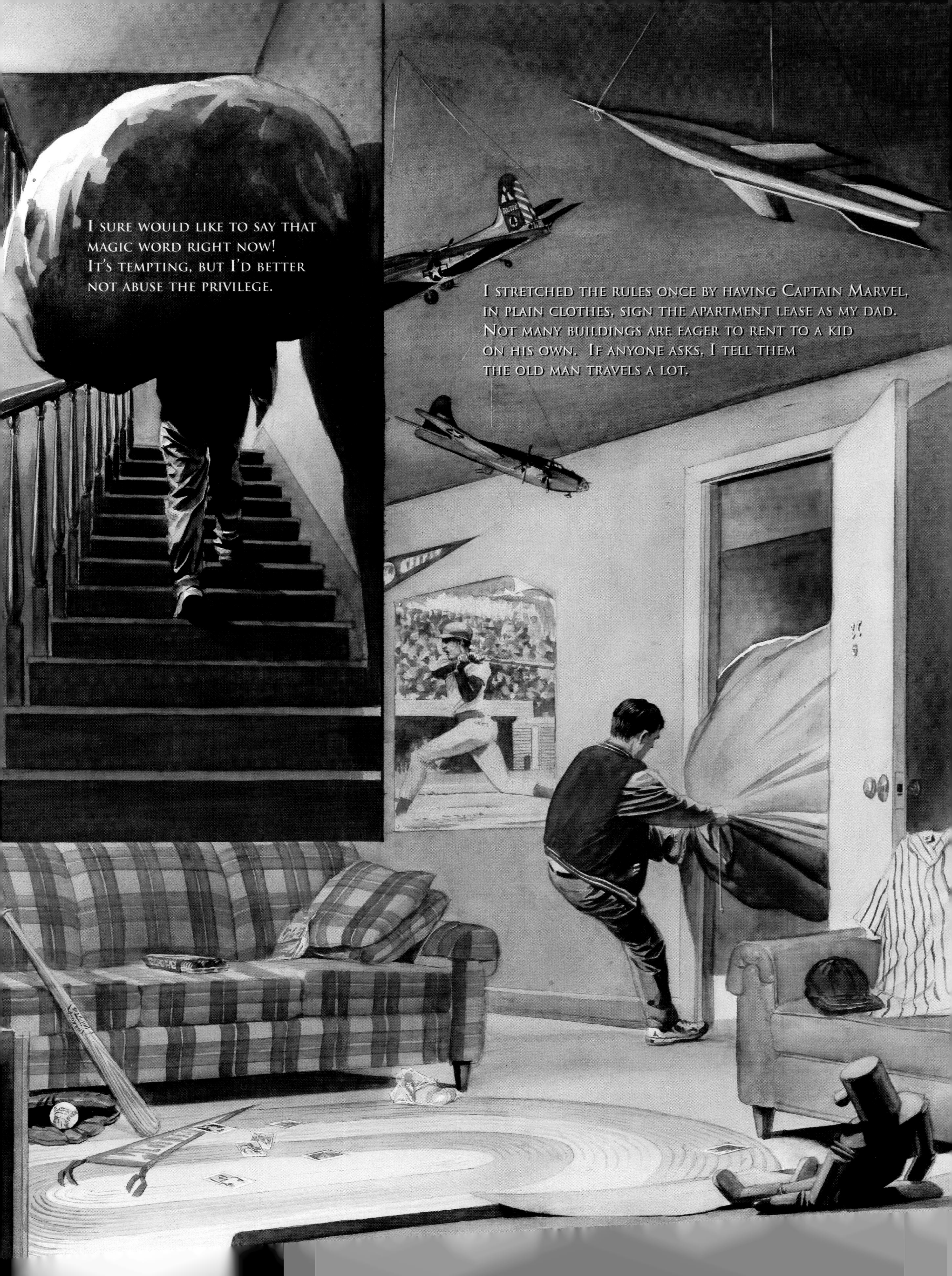
I sure would like to say that magic word right now! It's tempting, but I'd better not abuse the privilege.
I stretched the rules once by having Captain Marvel, in plain clothes, sign the apartment lease as my dad. Not many buildings are eager to rent to a kid on his own. If anyone asks, I tell them the old man travels a lot.

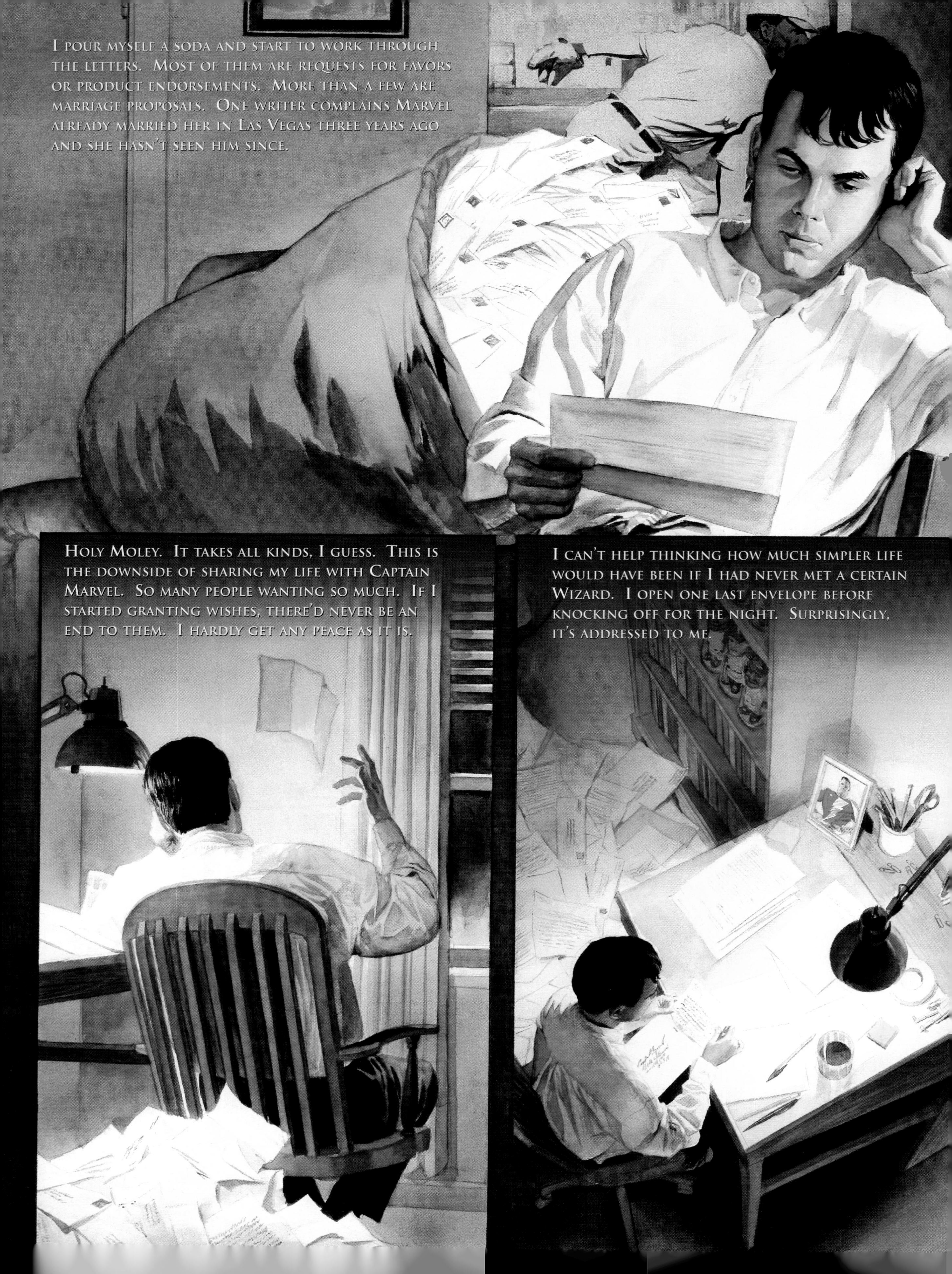
I pour myself a soda and start to work through the letters. Most of them are requests for favors or product endorsements. More than a few are marriage proposals. One writer complains Marvel already married her in Las Vegas three years ago and she hasn't seen him since.
Holy Moley. It takes all kinds, I guess. This is the downside of sharing my life with Captain Marvel. So many people wanting so much. If I started granting wishes, there'd never be an end to them. I hardly get any peace as it is.
I can't help thinking how much simpler life would have been if I had never met a certain Wizard. I open one last envelope before knocking off for the night. Surprisingly, it's addressed to me.

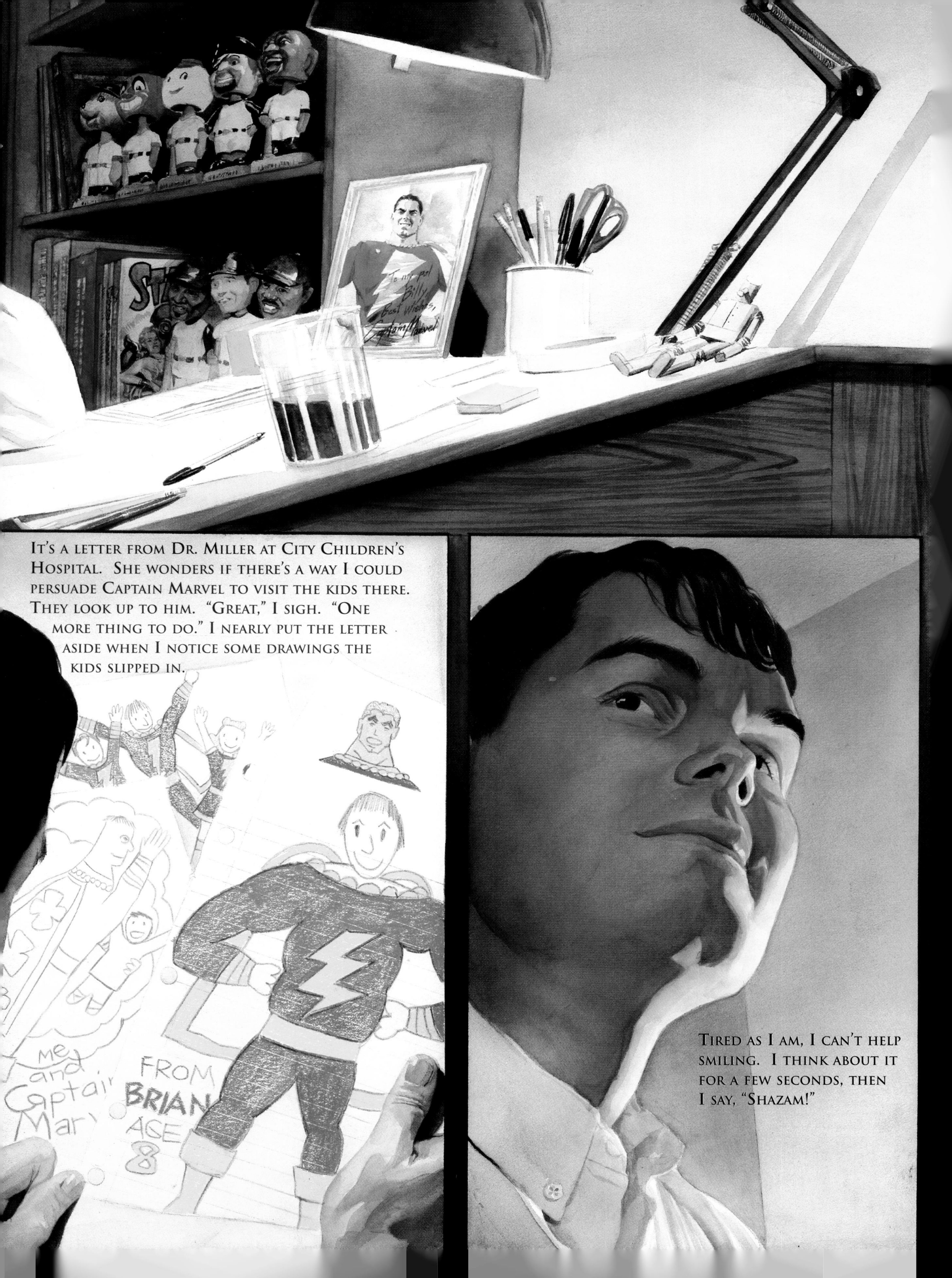

It's a letter from Dr. Miller at City Children's Hospital. She wonders if there's a way I could persuade Captain Marvel to visit the kids there. They look up to him. "Great," I sigh. "One more thing to do." I nearly put the letter aside when I notice some drawings the kids slipped in.
me and
FROM BRIAN AGE 8
Tired as I am, I can't help smiling. I think about it for a few seconds, then I say, "Shazam!"

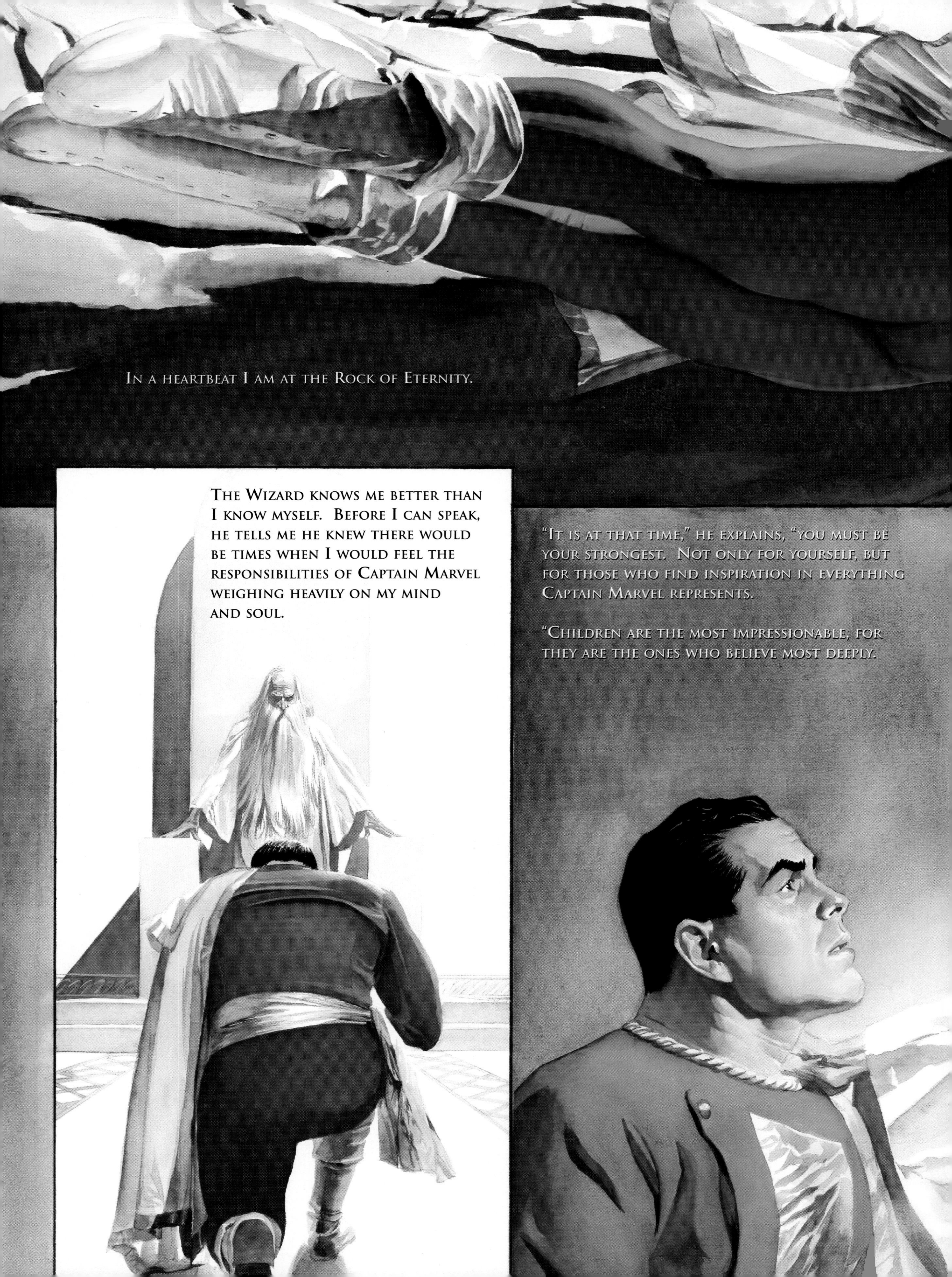
In a heartbeat I am at the Rock of Eternity.
The Wizard knows me better than I know myself. Before I can speak, he tells me he knew there would be times when I would feel the responsibilities of Captain Marvel weighing heavily on my mind and soul.
"It is at that time," he explains, "you must be your strongest. Not only for yourself, but for those who find inspiration in everything Captain Marvel represents.
"Children are the most impressionable, for they are the ones who believe most deeply.

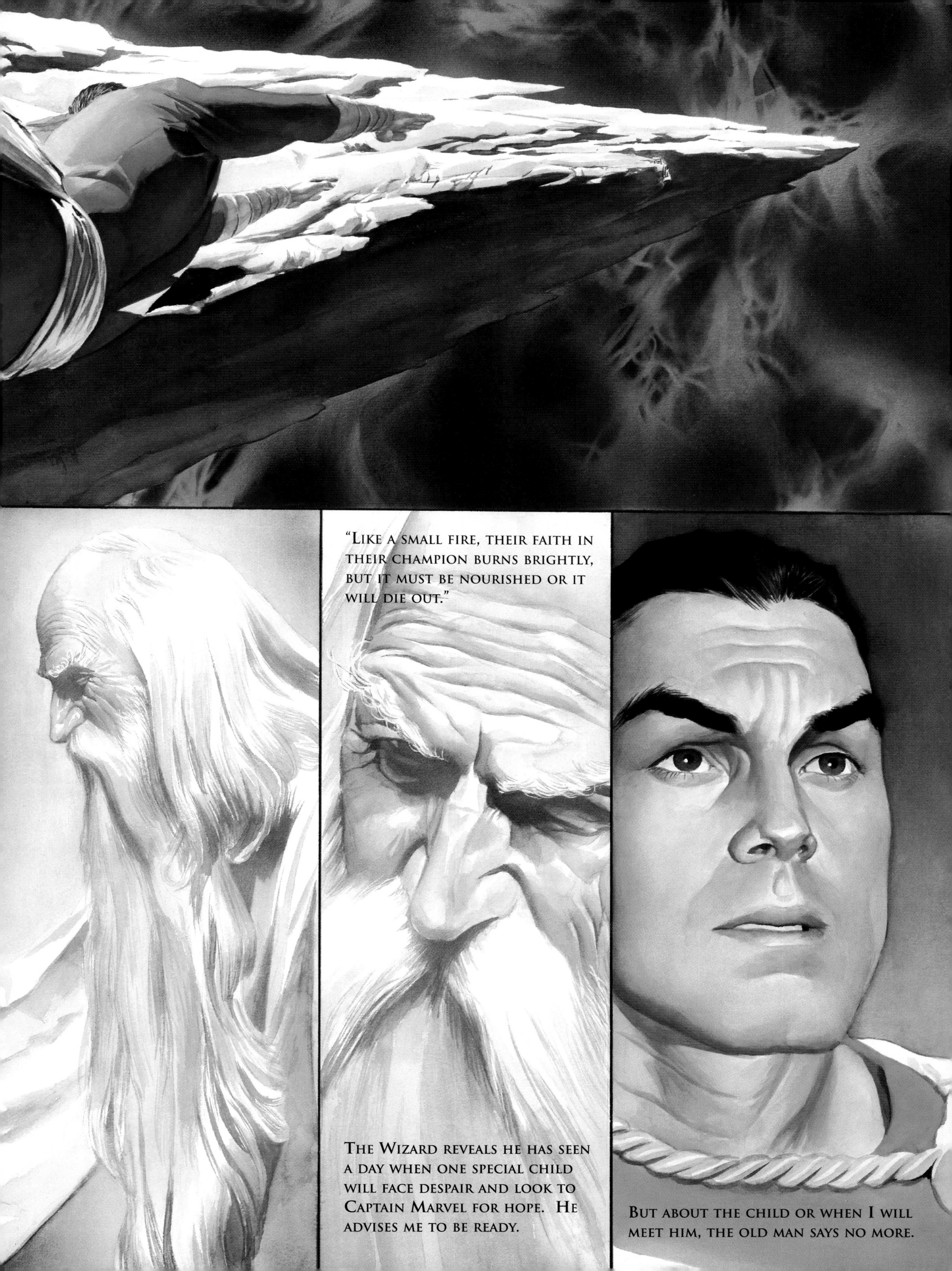
"LIKE A SMALL FIRE, THEIR FAITH IN THEIR CHAMPION BURNS BRIGHTLY, BUT IT MUST BE NOURISHED OR IT WILL DIE OUT."
THE WIZARD REVEALS HE HAS SEEN A DAY WHEN ONE SPECIAL CHILD WILL FACE DESPAIR AND LOOK TO CAPTAIN MARVEL FOR HOPE. HE ADVISES ME TO BE READY.
BUT ABOUT THE CHILD OR WHEN I WILL MEET HIM, THE OLD MAN SAYS NO MORE.

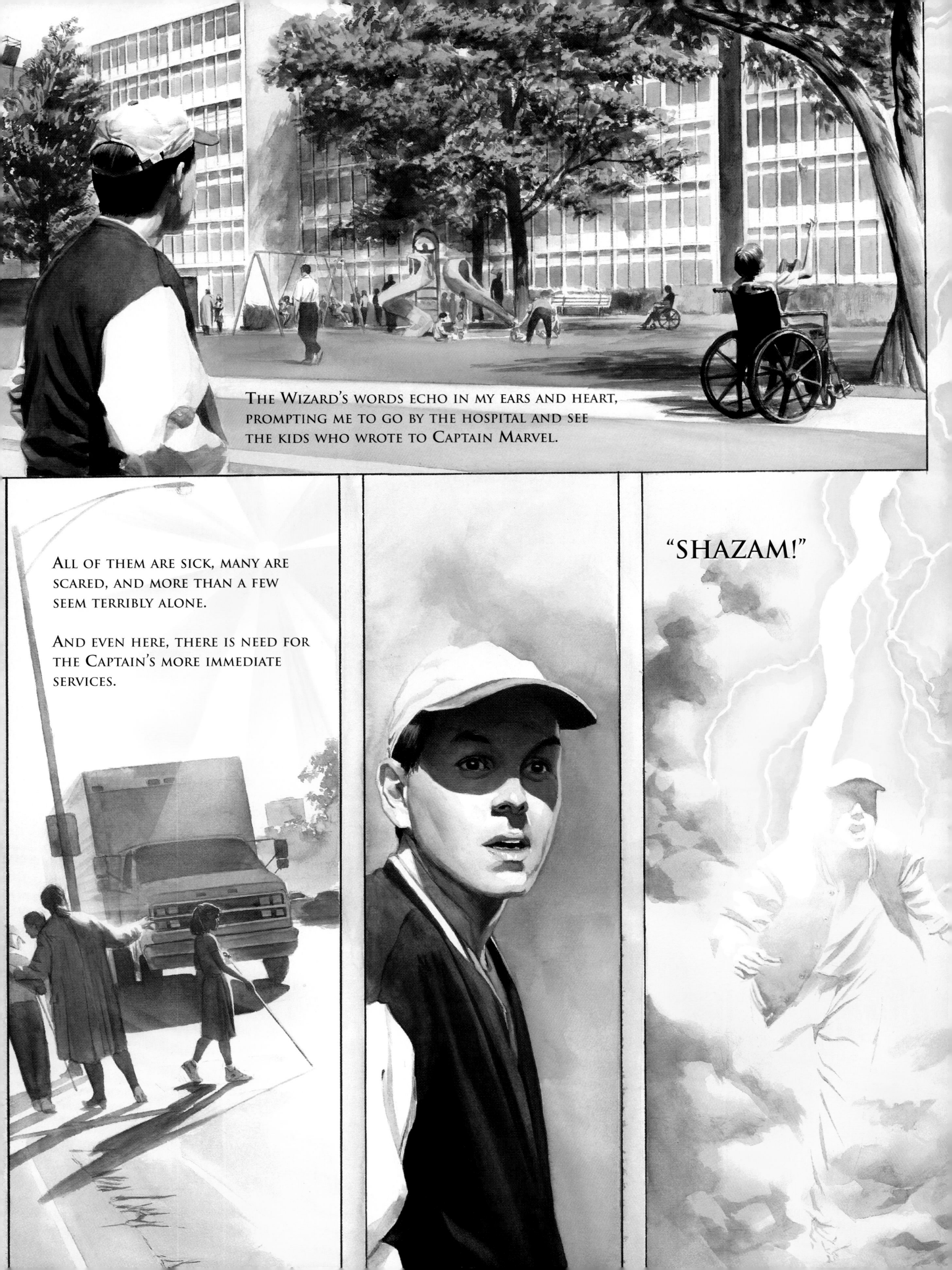
The Wizard's words echo in my ears and heart, prompting me to go by the hospital and see the kids who wrote to Captain Marvel.
All of them are sick, many are scared, and more than a few seem terribly alone.
And even here, there is need for the Captain's more immediate services.
"SHAZAM!"

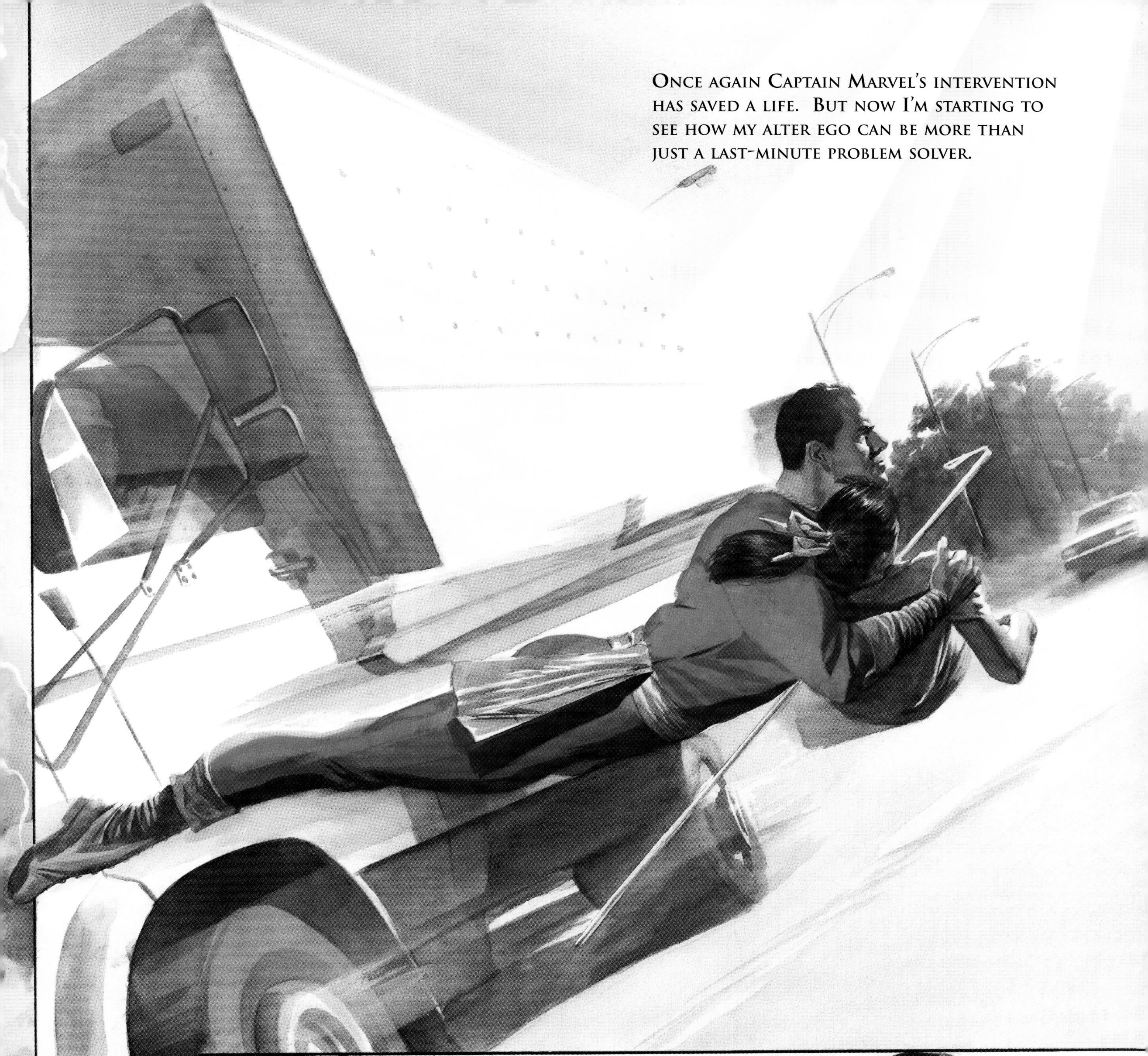
Once again Captain Marvel's intervention has saved a life. But now I'm starting to see how my alter ego can be more than just a last-minute problem solver.

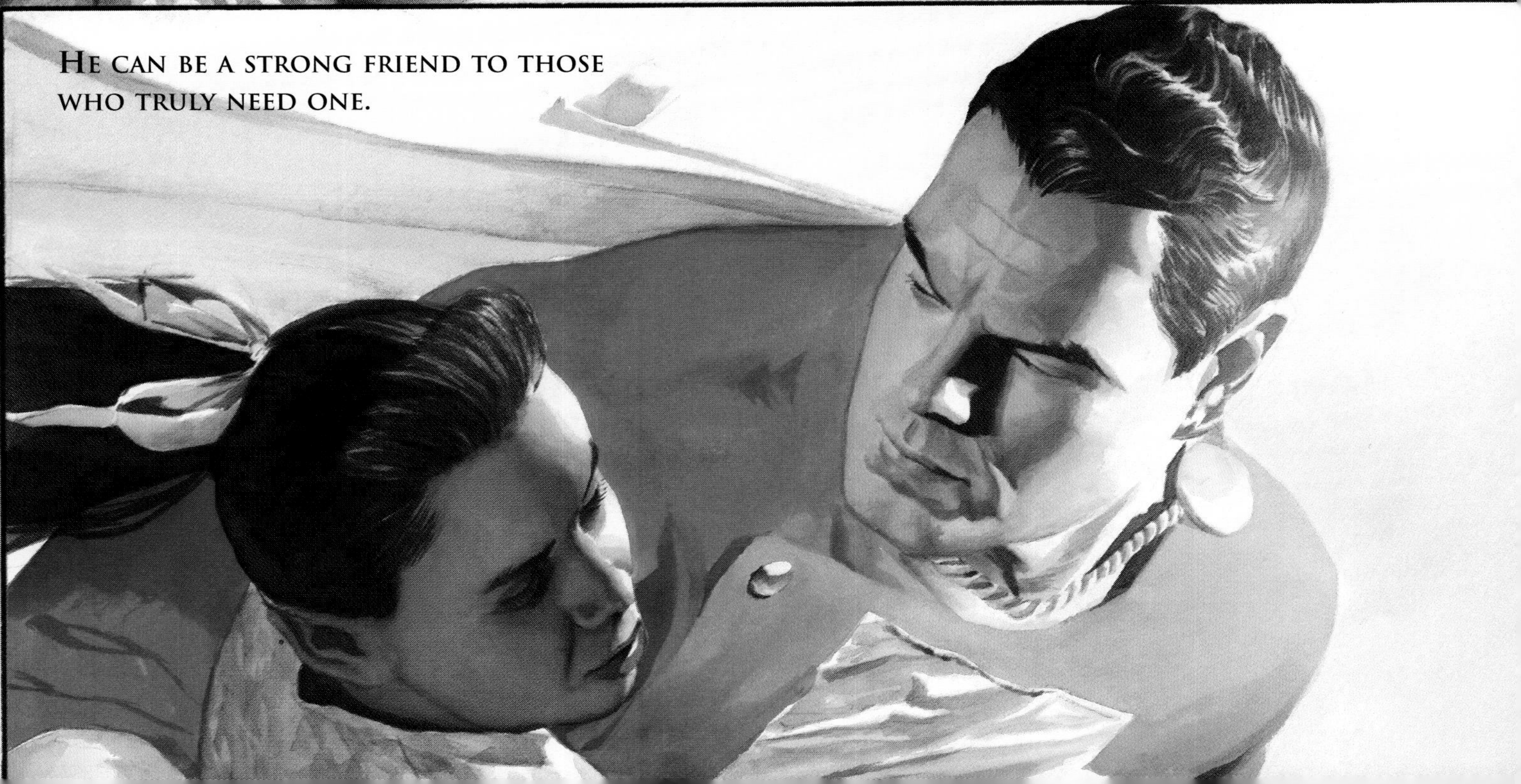
He can be a strong friend to those who truly need one.

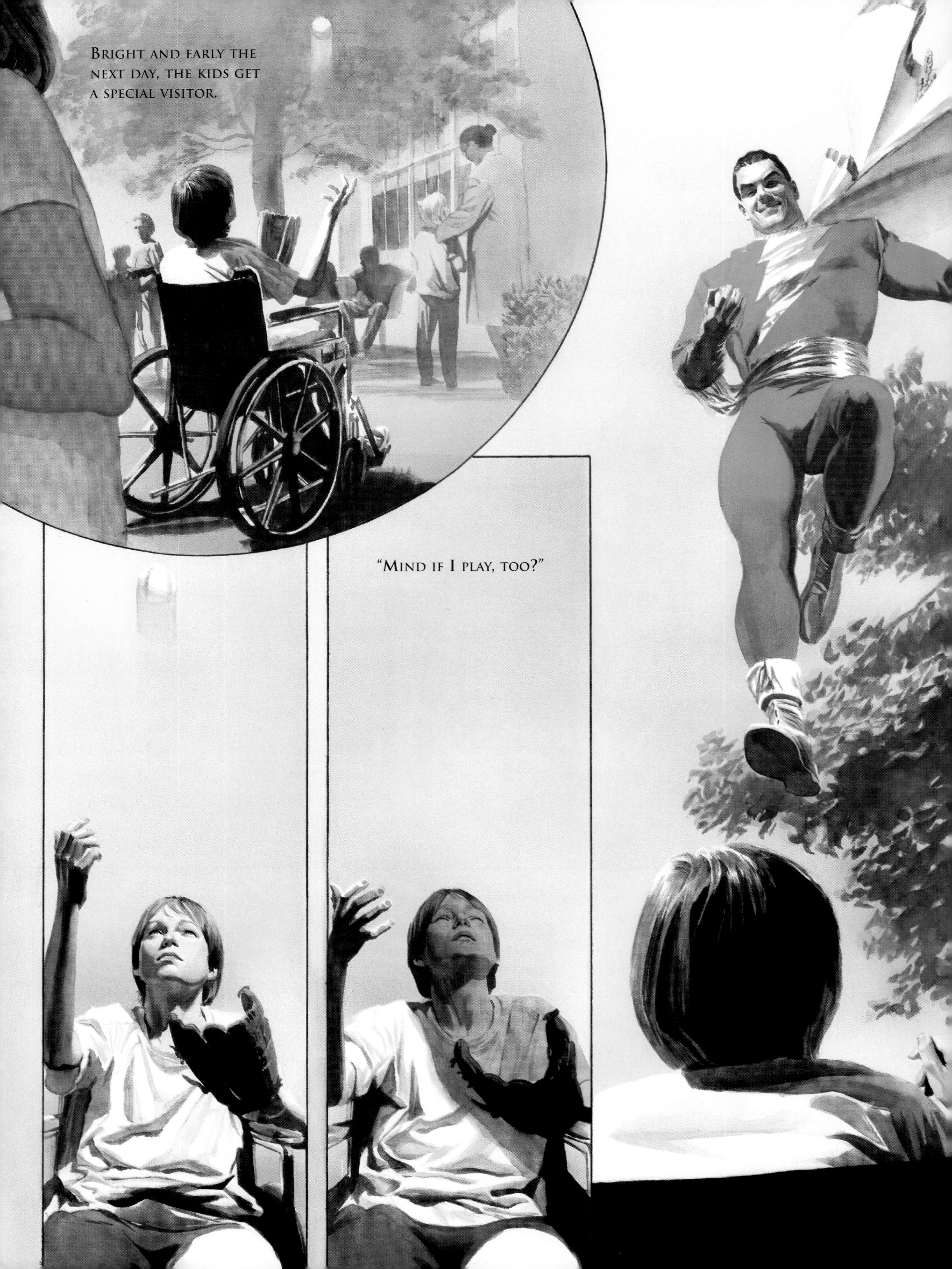
Bright and early the next day, the kids get a special visitor.
"Mind if I play, too?"

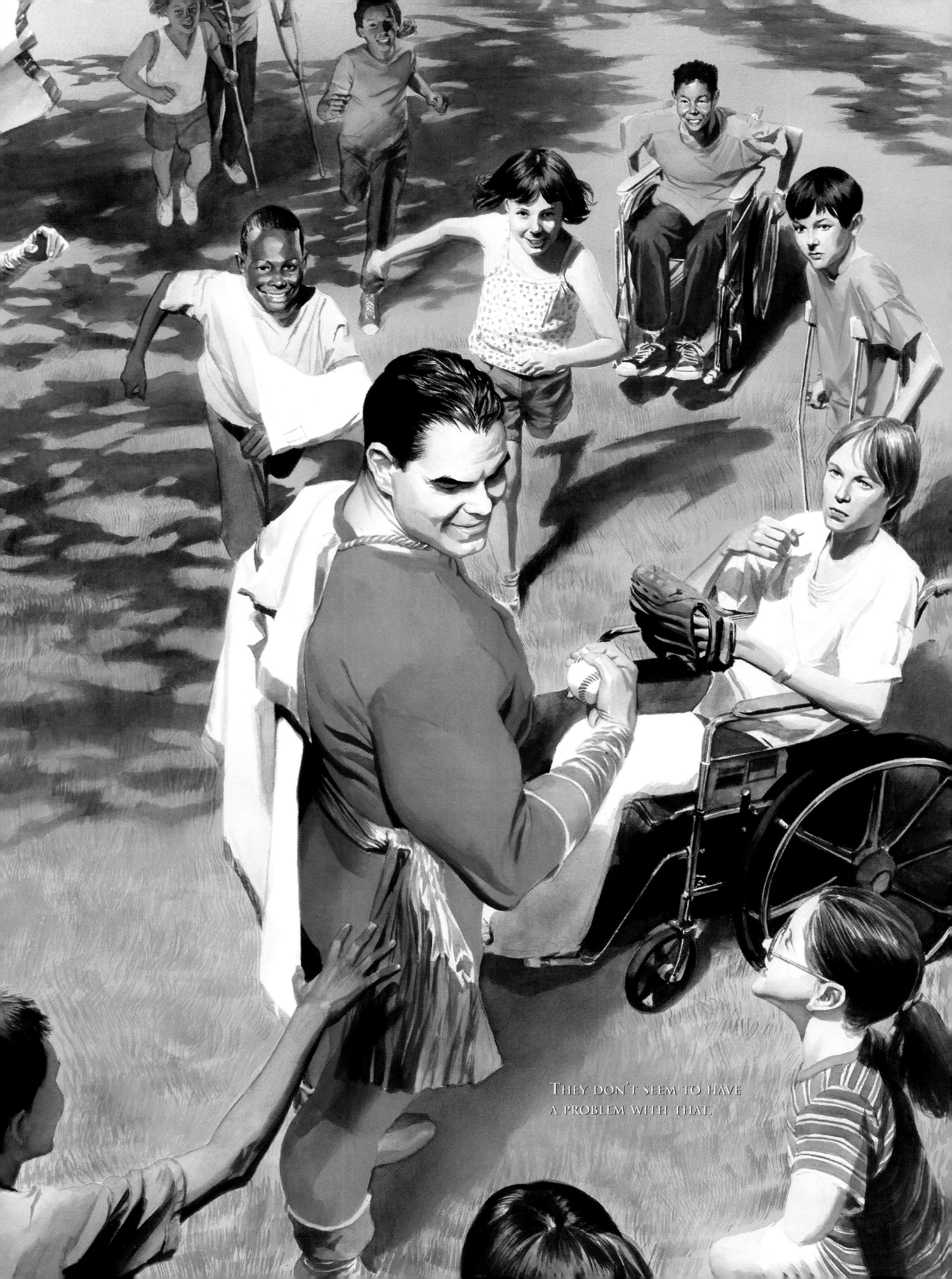
They don't seem to have a problem with that.

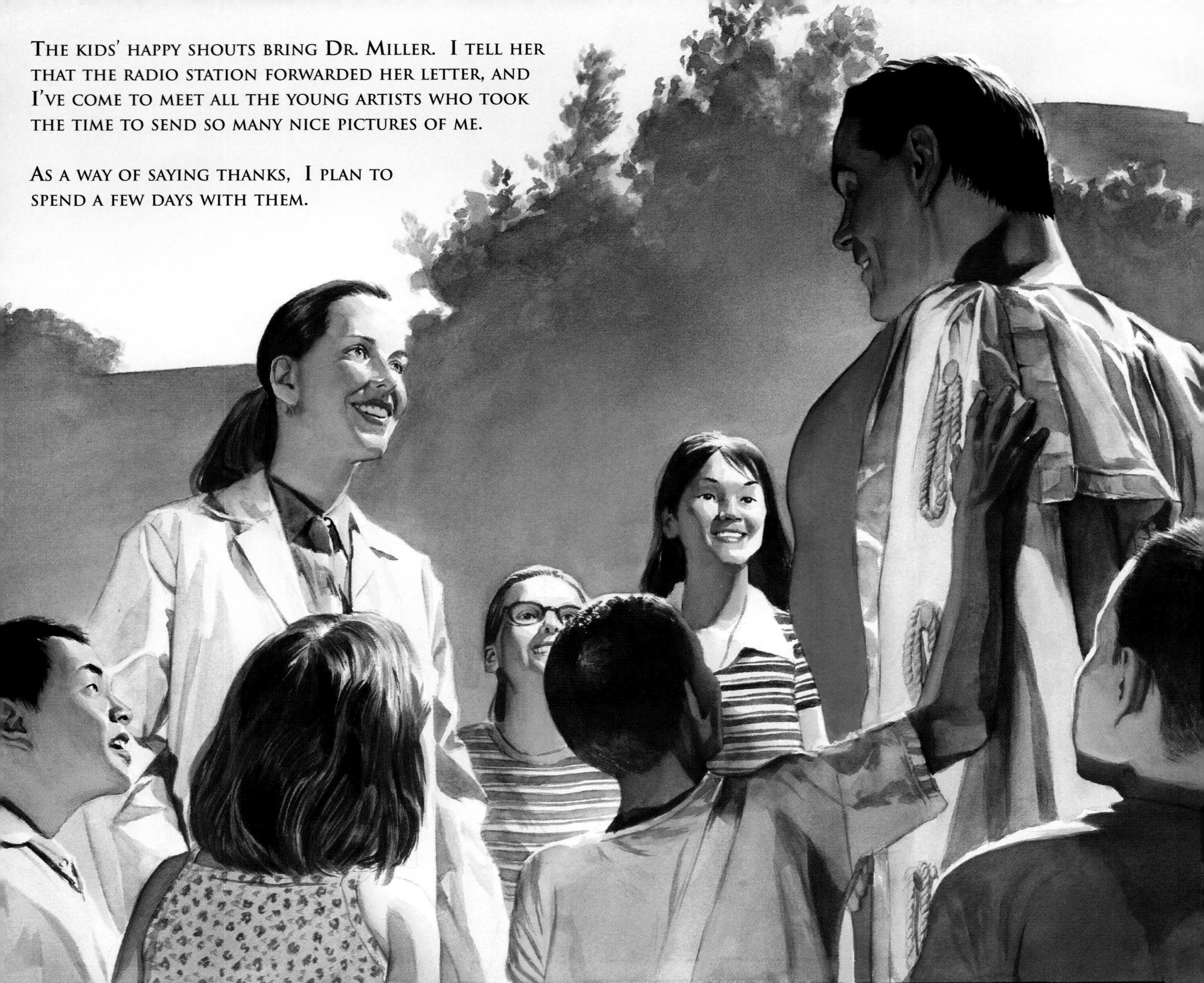
The kids' happy shouts bring Dr. Miller. I tell her that the radio station forwarded her letter, and I've come to meet all the young artists who took the time to send so many nice pictures of me.
As a way of saying thanks, I plan to spend a few days with them.

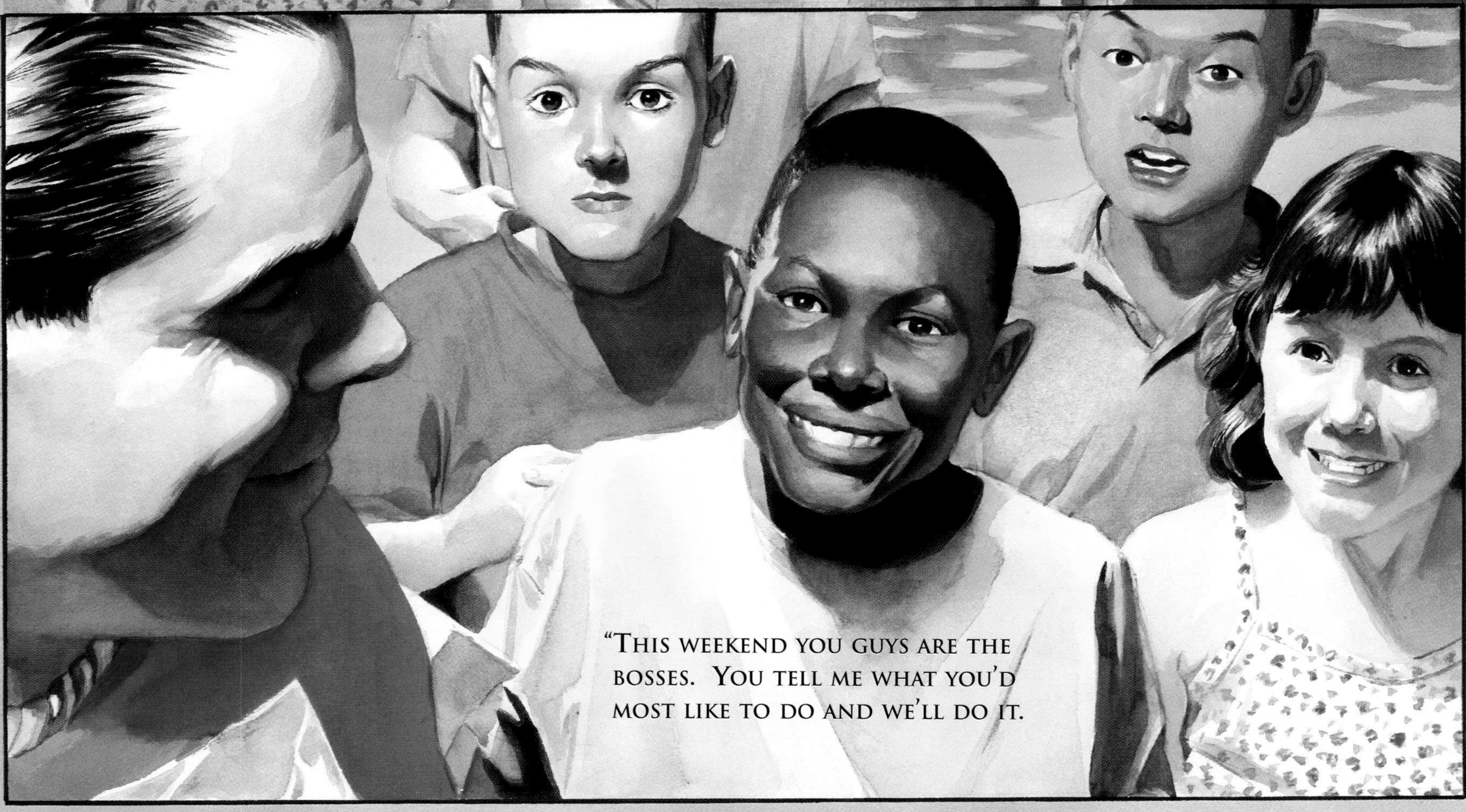
"This weekend you guys are the bosses. You tell me what you'd most like to do and we'll do it.

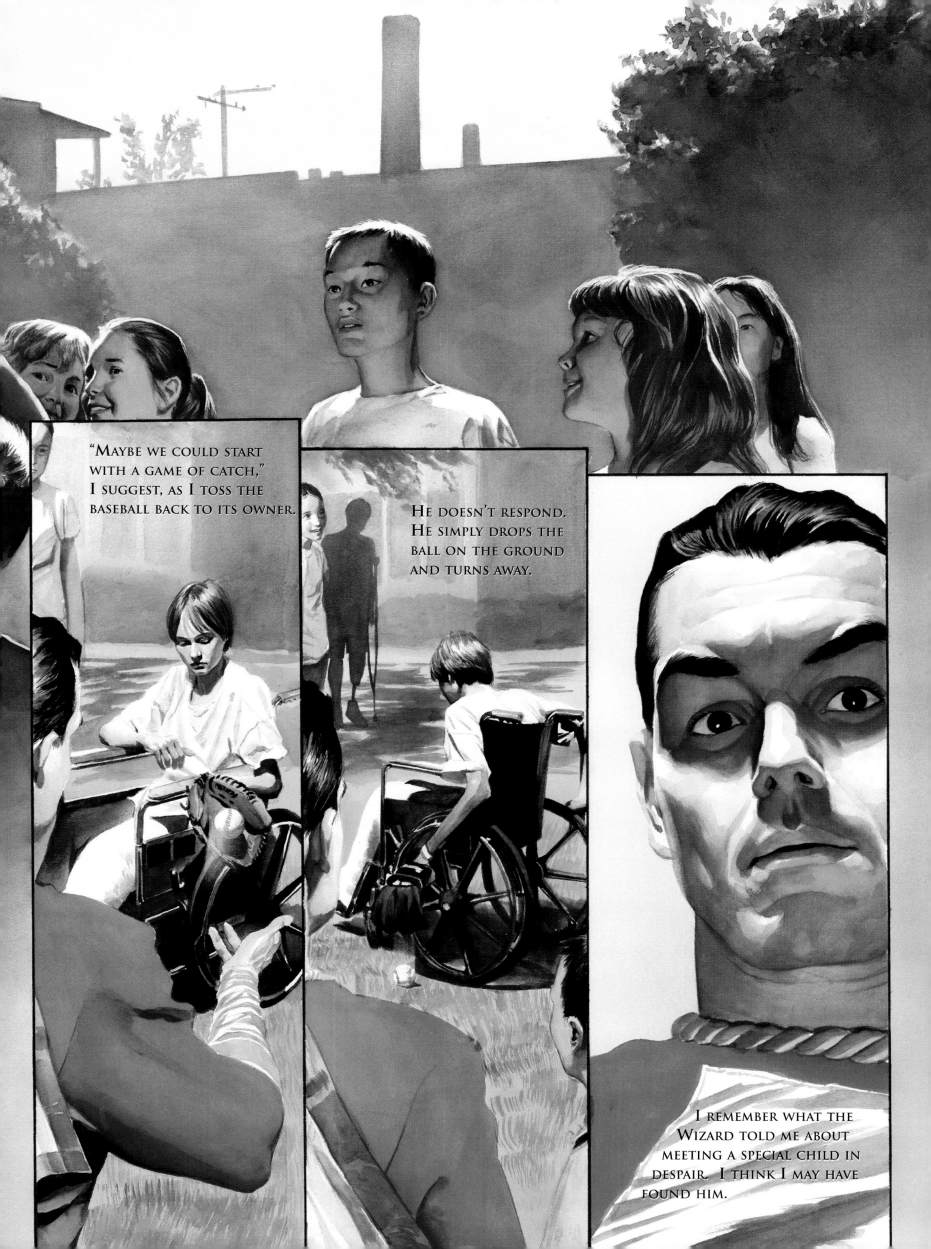

"MAYBE WE COULD START WITH A GAME OF CATCH," I SUGGEST, AS I TOSS THE BASEBALL BACK TO ITS OWNER.

HE DOESN'T RESPOND. HE SIMPLY DROPS THE BALL ON THE GROUND AND TURNS AWAY.

I REMEMBER WHAT THE WIZARD TOLD ME ABOUT MEETING A SPECIAL CHILD IN DESPAIR. I THINK I MAY HAVE FOUND HIM.

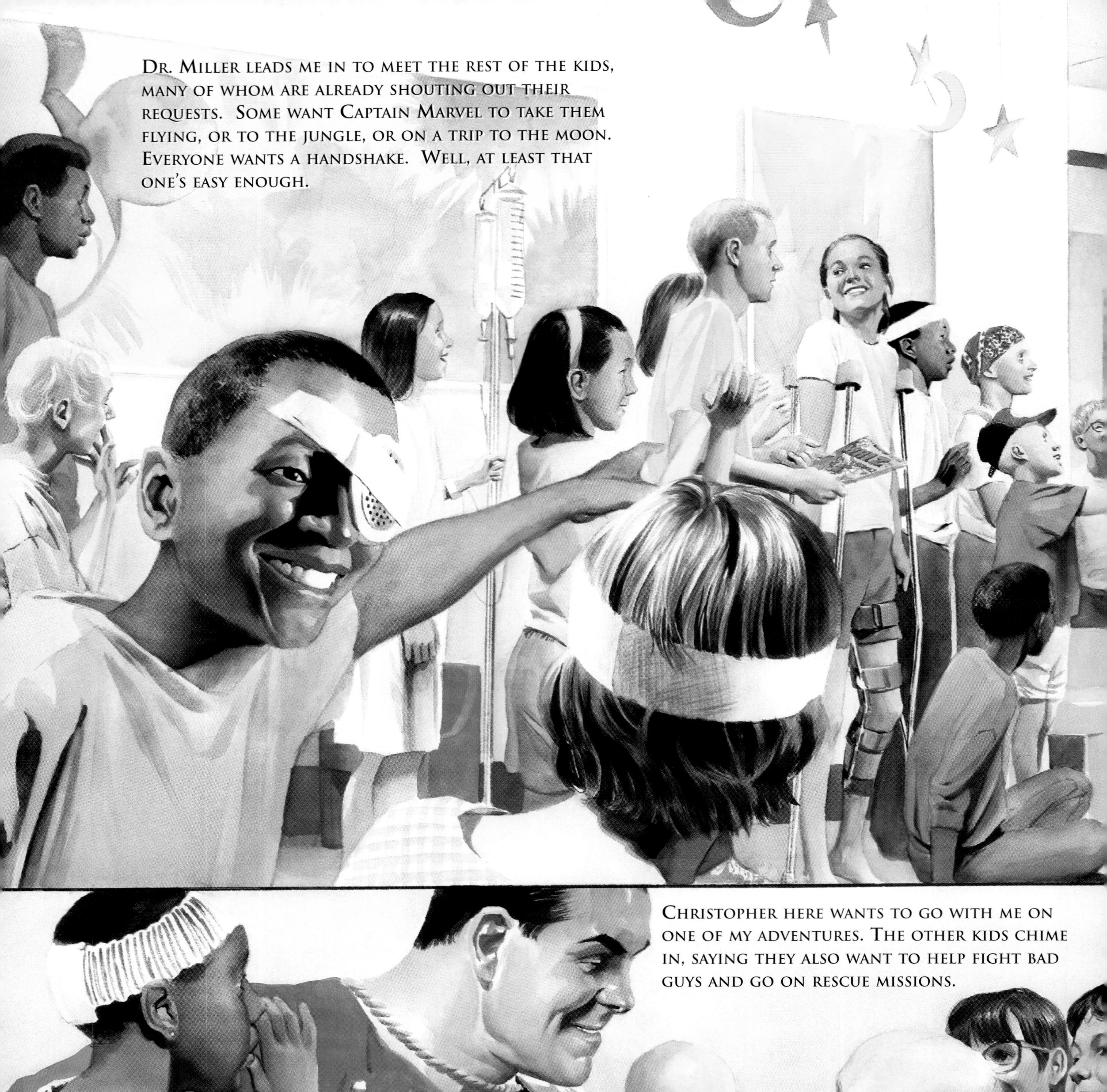
Dr. Miller leads me in to meet the rest of the kids, many of whom are already shouting out their requests. Some want Captain Marvel to take them flying, or to the jungle, or on a trip to the moon. Everyone wants a handshake. Well, at least that one's easy enough.

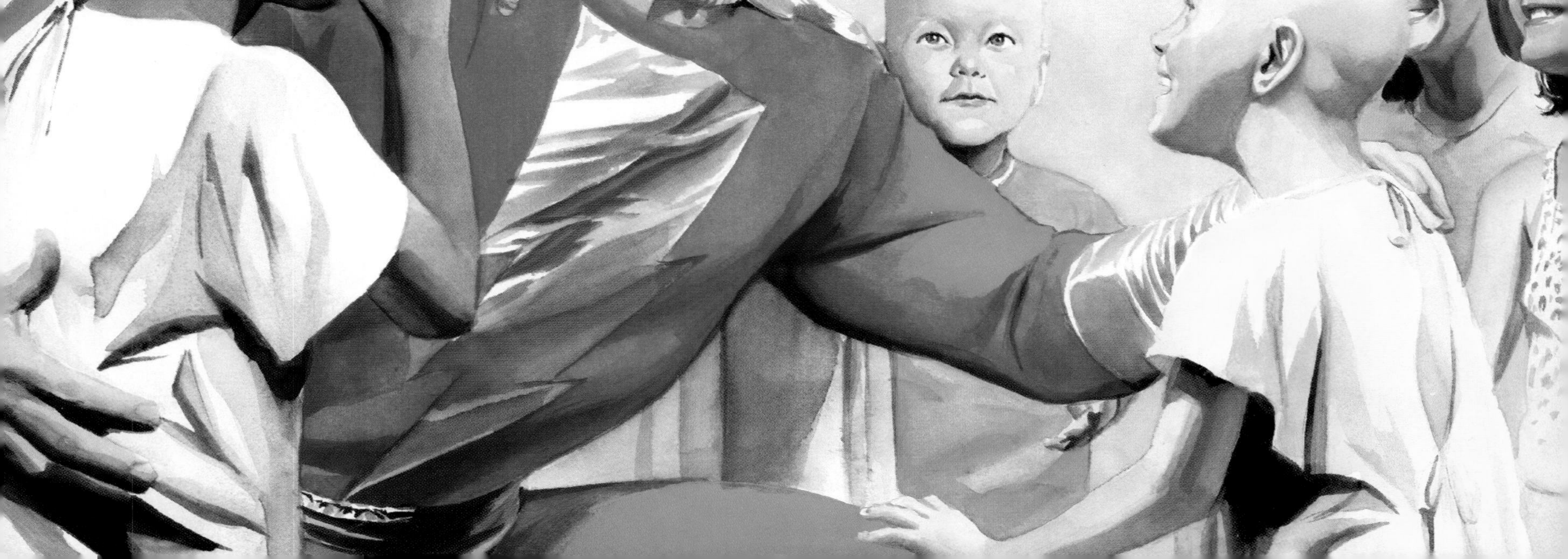
Christopher here wants to go with me on one of my adventures. The other kids chime in, saying they also want to help fight bad guys and go on rescue missions.

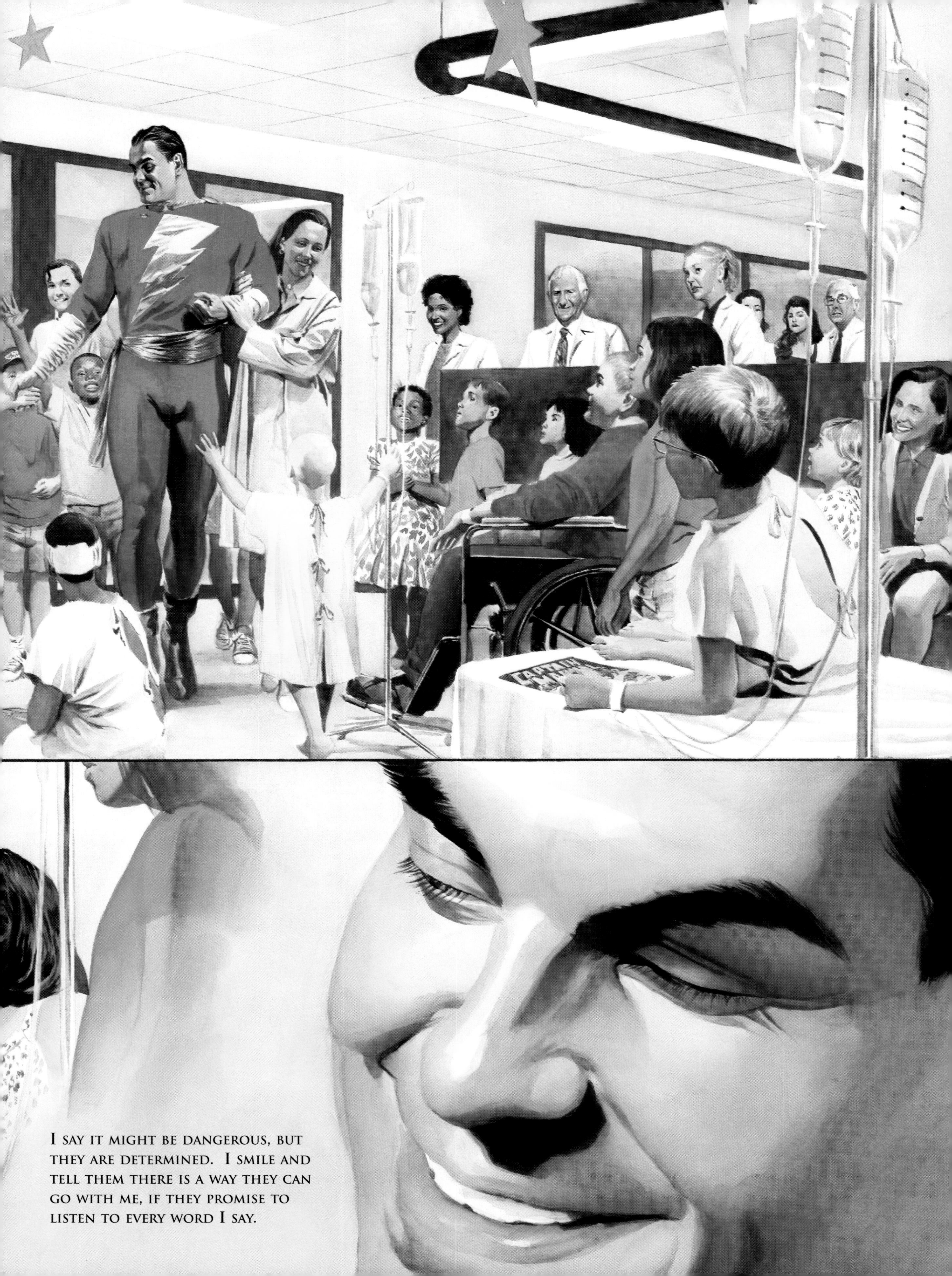
I SAY IT MIGHT BE DANGEROUS, BUT THEY ARE DETERMINED. I SMILE AND TELL THEM THERE IS A WAY THEY CAN GO WITH ME, IF THEY PROMISE TO LISTEN TO EVERY WORD I SAY.

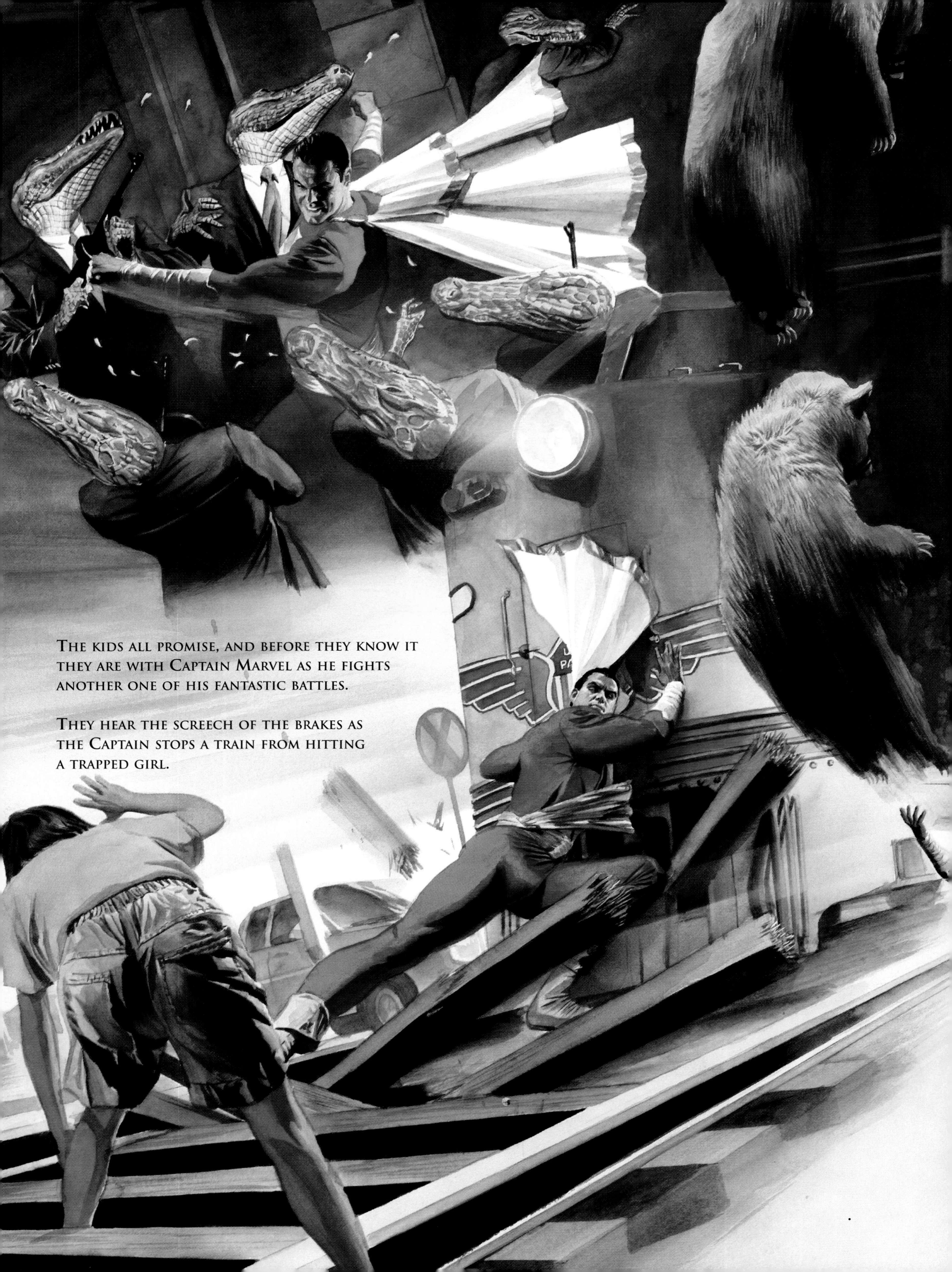

The kids all promise, and before they know it they are with Captain Marvel as he fights another one of his fantastic battles.

They hear the screech of the brakes as the Captain stops a train from hitting a trapped girl.

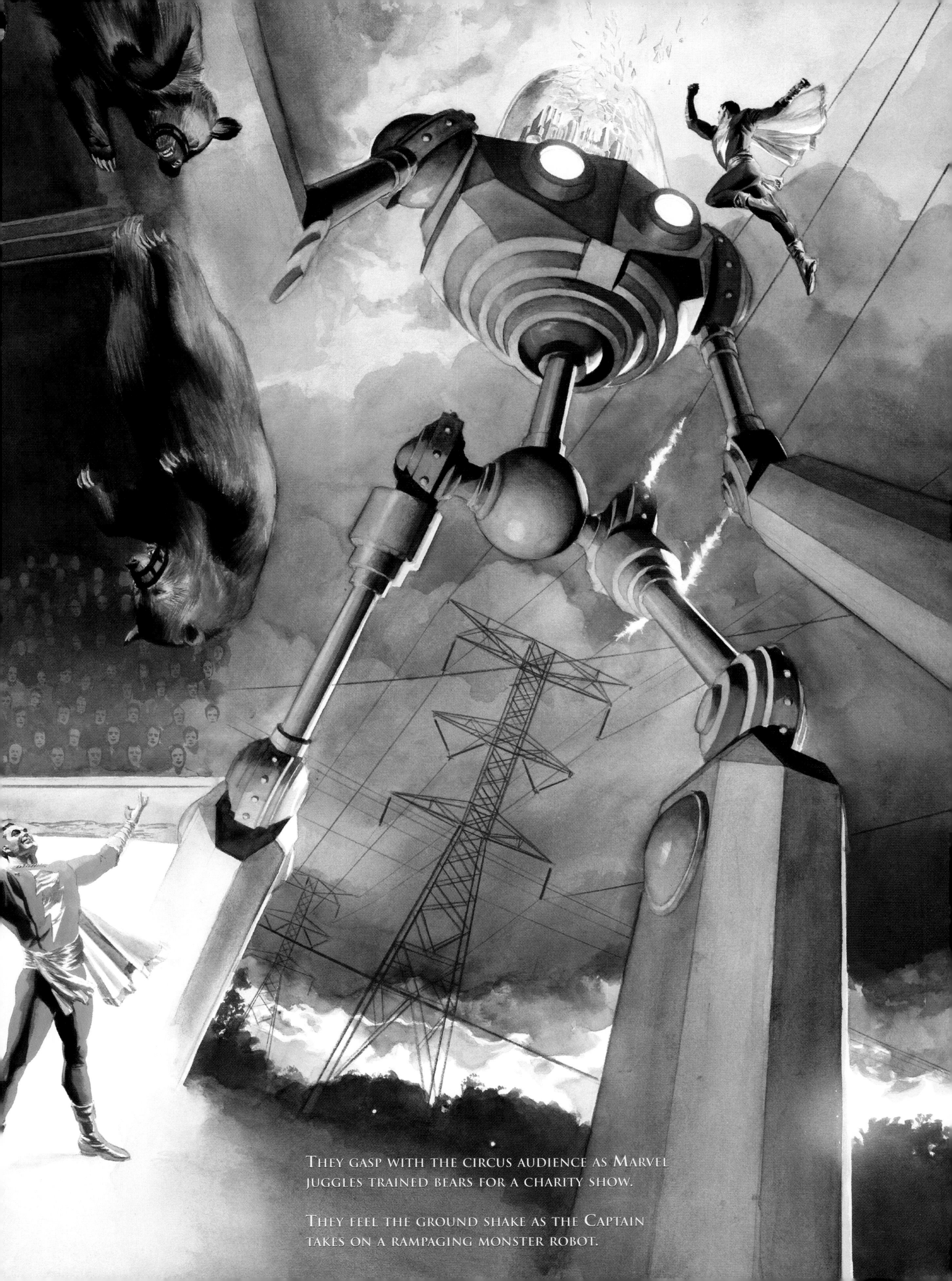
They gasp with the circus audience as Marvel juggles trained bears for a charity show.
They feel the ground shake as the Captain takes on a rampaging monster robot.

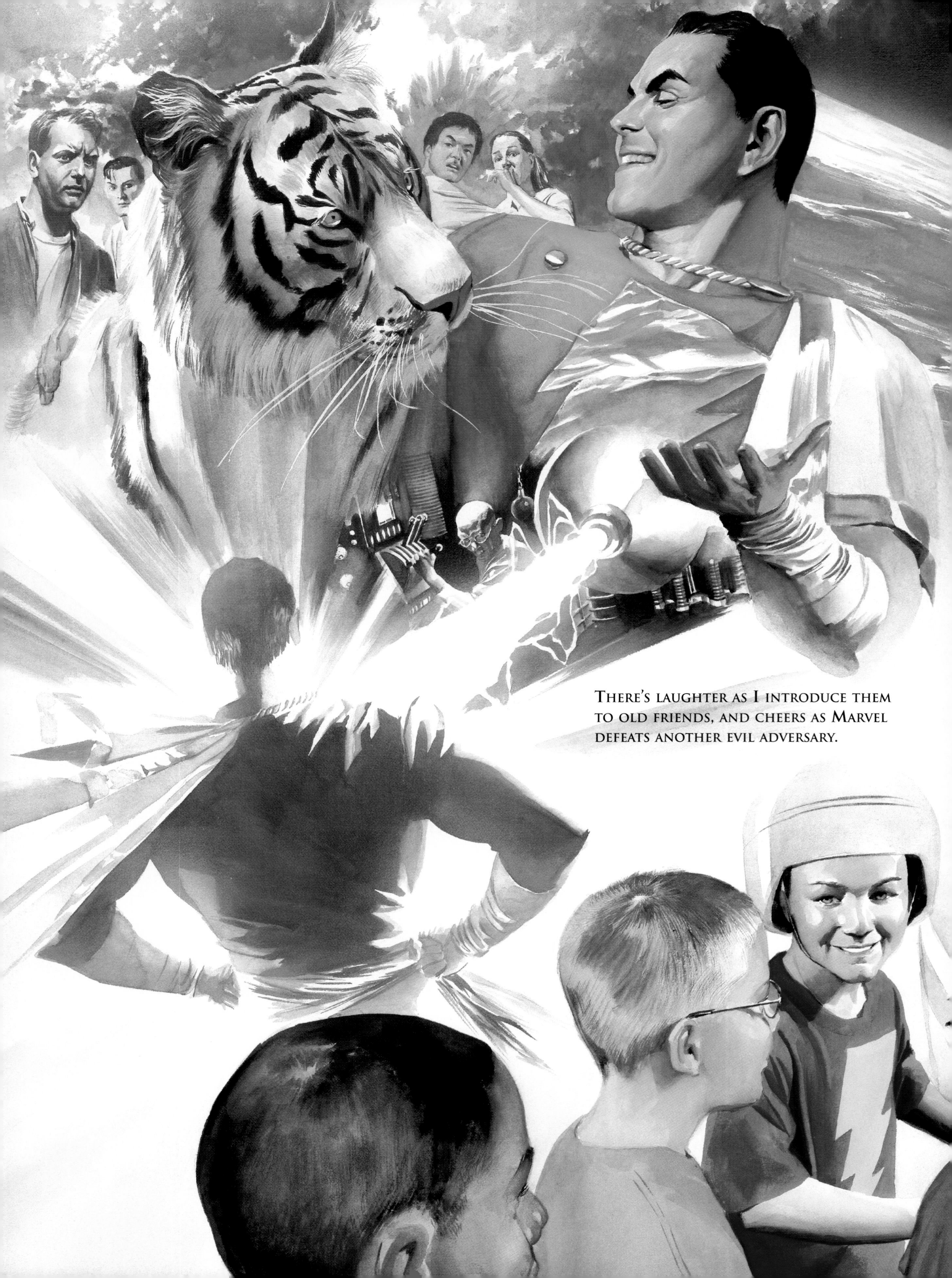

There's laughter as I introduce them to old friends, and cheers as Marvel defeats another evil adversary.

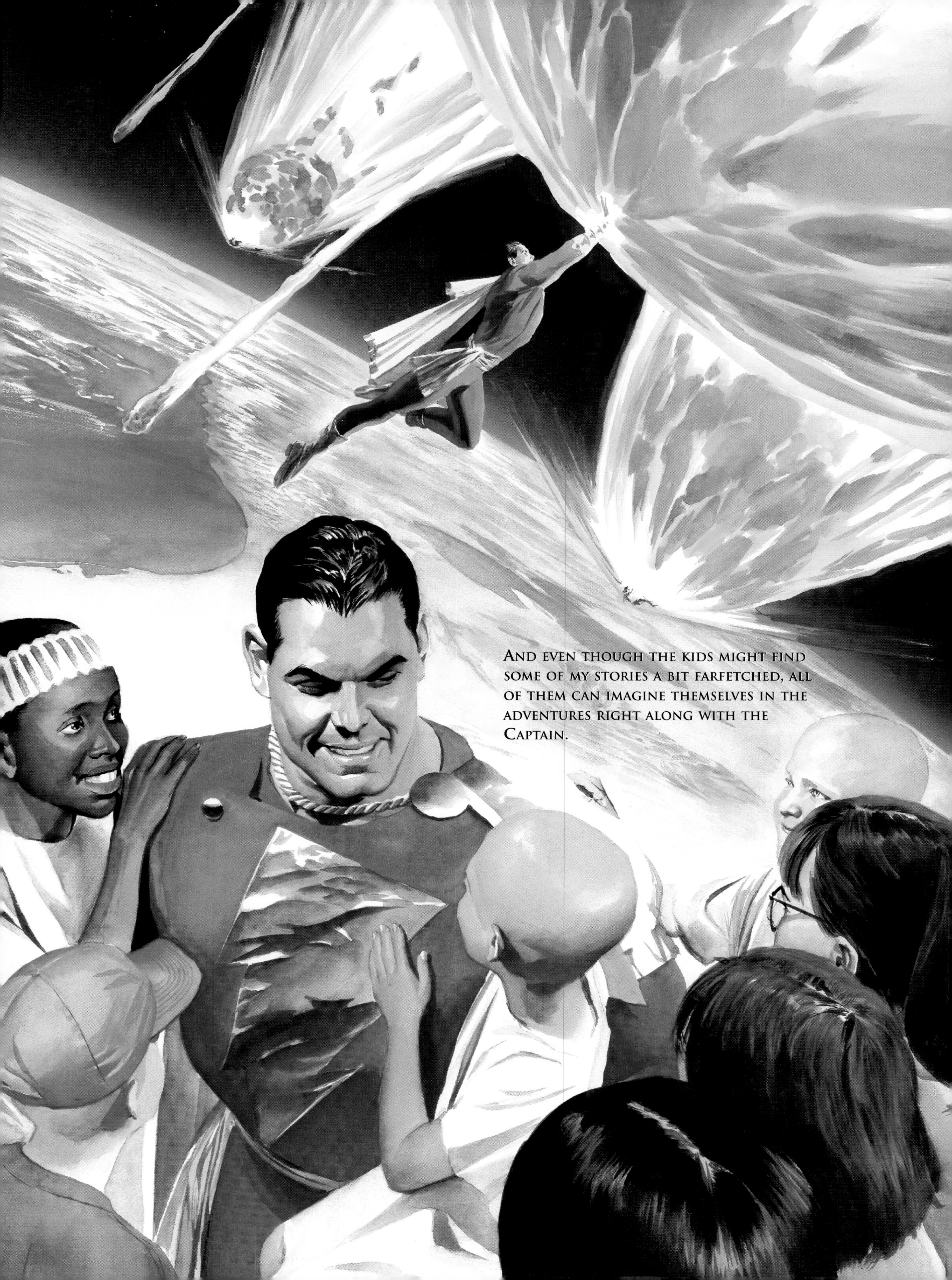
AND EVEN THOUGH THE KIDS MIGHT FIND SOME OF MY STORIES A BIT FARFETCHED, ALL OF THEM CAN IMAGINE THEMSELVES IN THE ADVENTURES RIGHT ALONG WITH THE CAPTAIN.

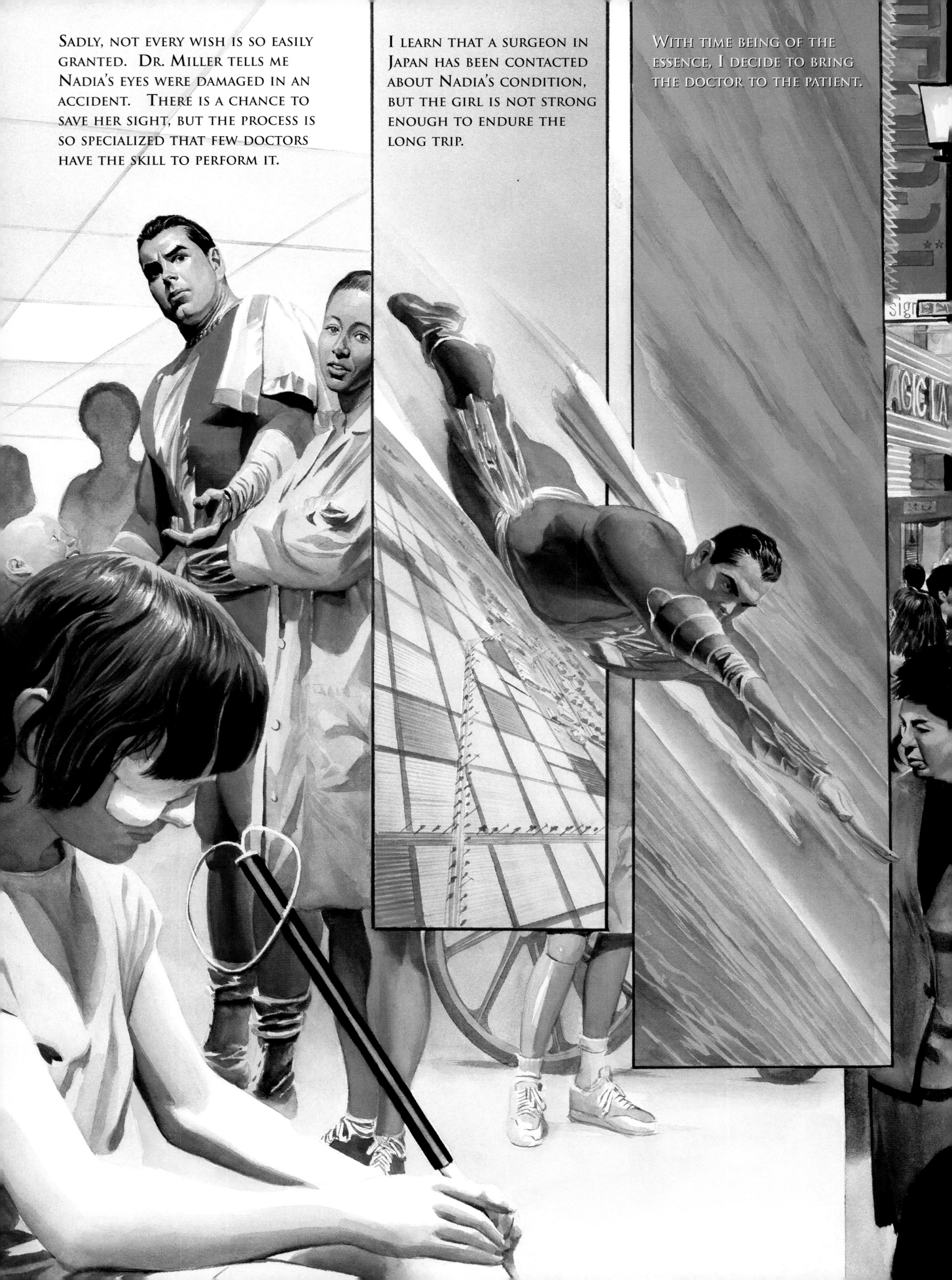
Sadly, not every wish is so easily granted. Dr. Miller tells me Nadia's eyes were damaged in an accident. There is a chance to save her sight, but the process is so specialized that few doctors have the skill to perform it.
I learn that a surgeon in Japan has been contacted about Nadia's condition, but the girl is not strong enough to endure the long trip.
With time being of the essence, I decide to bring the doctor to the patient.

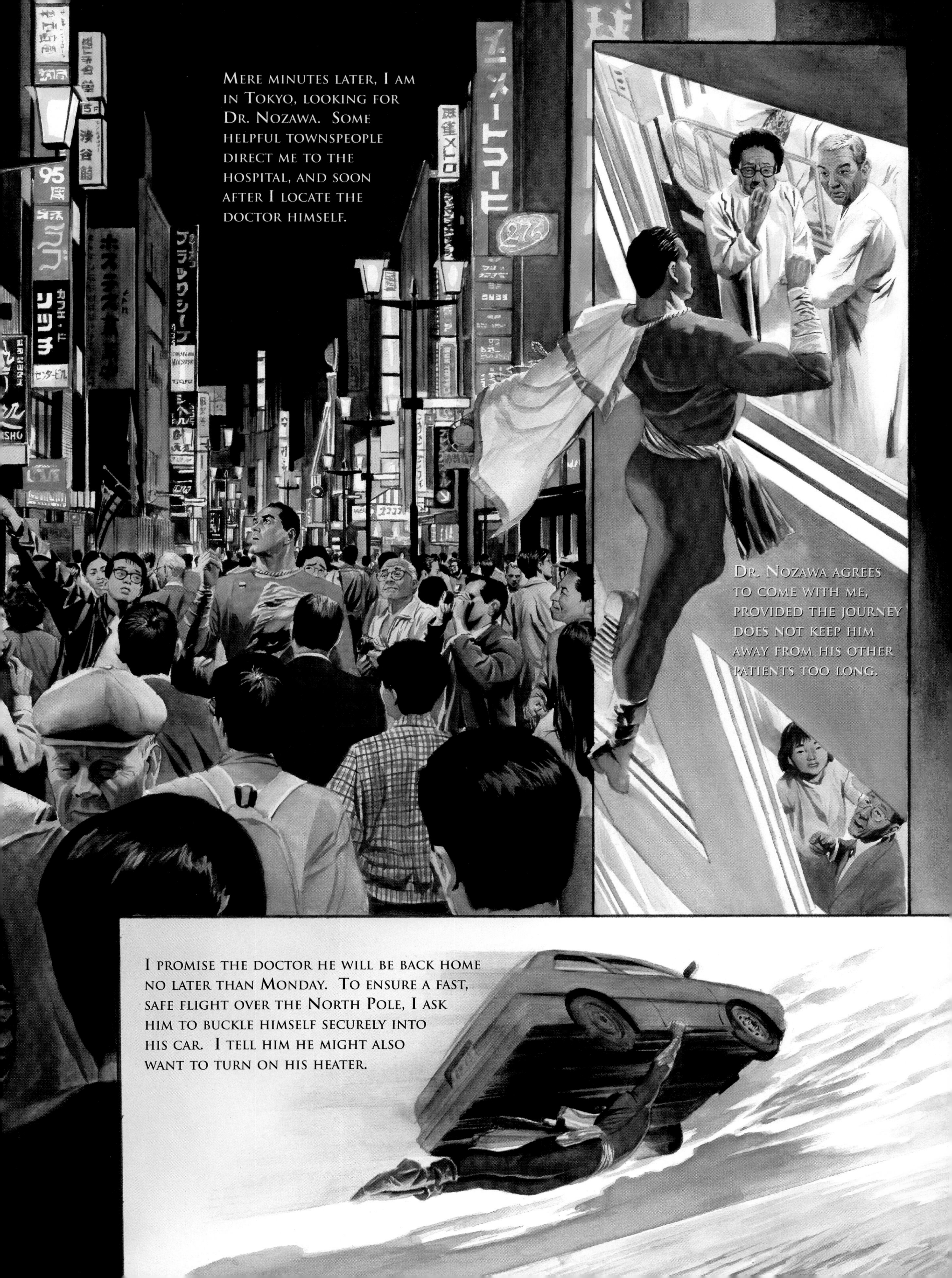
Mere minutes later, I am in Tokyo, looking for Dr. Nozawa. Some helpful townspeople direct me to the hospital, and soon after I locate the doctor himself.
Dr. Nozawa agrees to come with me, provided the journey does not keep him away from his other patients too long.
I promise the doctor he will be back home no later than Monday. To ensure a fast, safe flight over the North Pole, I ask him to buckle himself securely into his car. I tell him he might also want to turn on his heater.

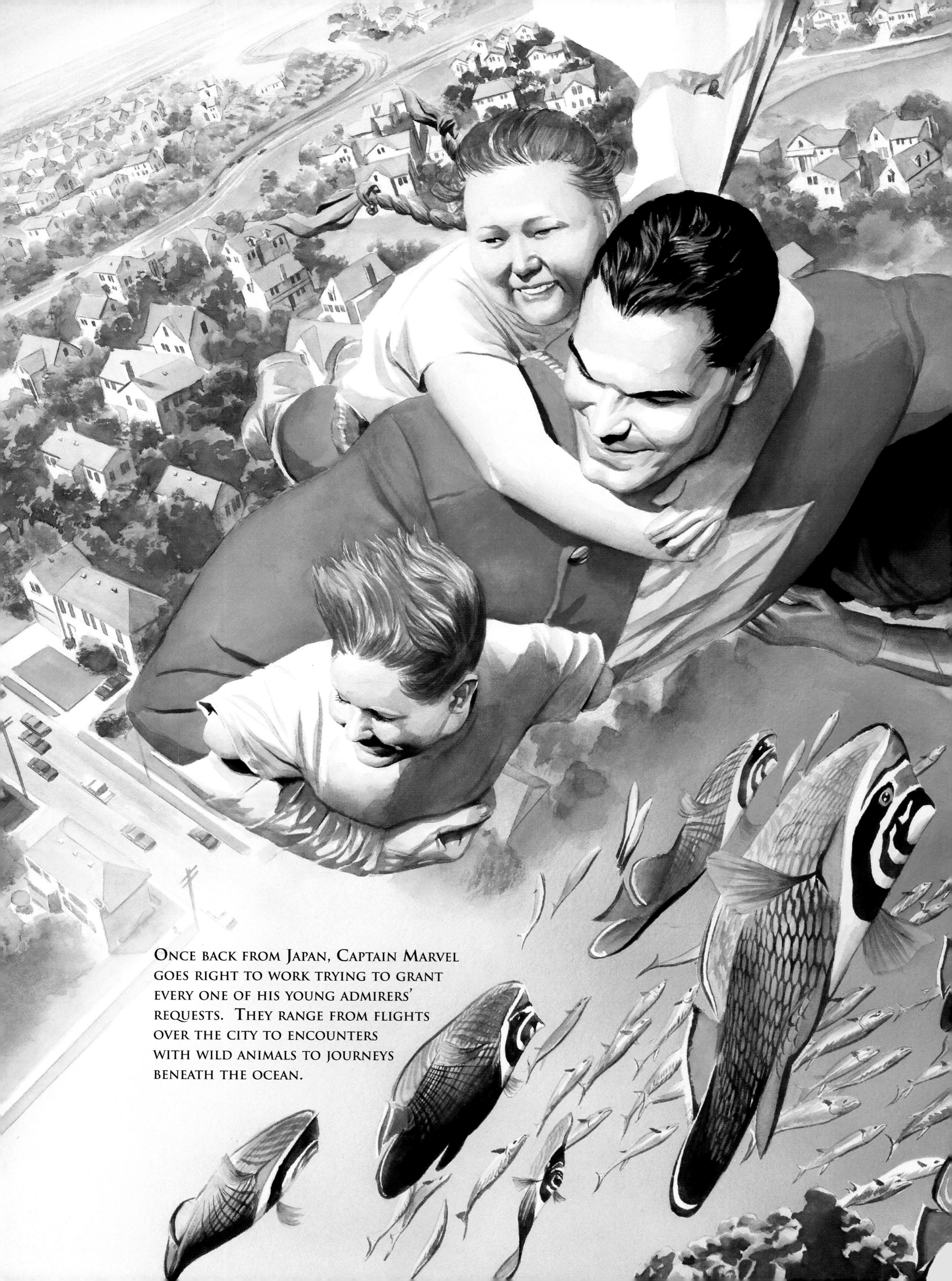

Once back from Japan, Captain Marvel goes right to work trying to grant every one of his young admirers' requests. They range from flights over the city to encounters with wild animals to journeys beneath the ocean.

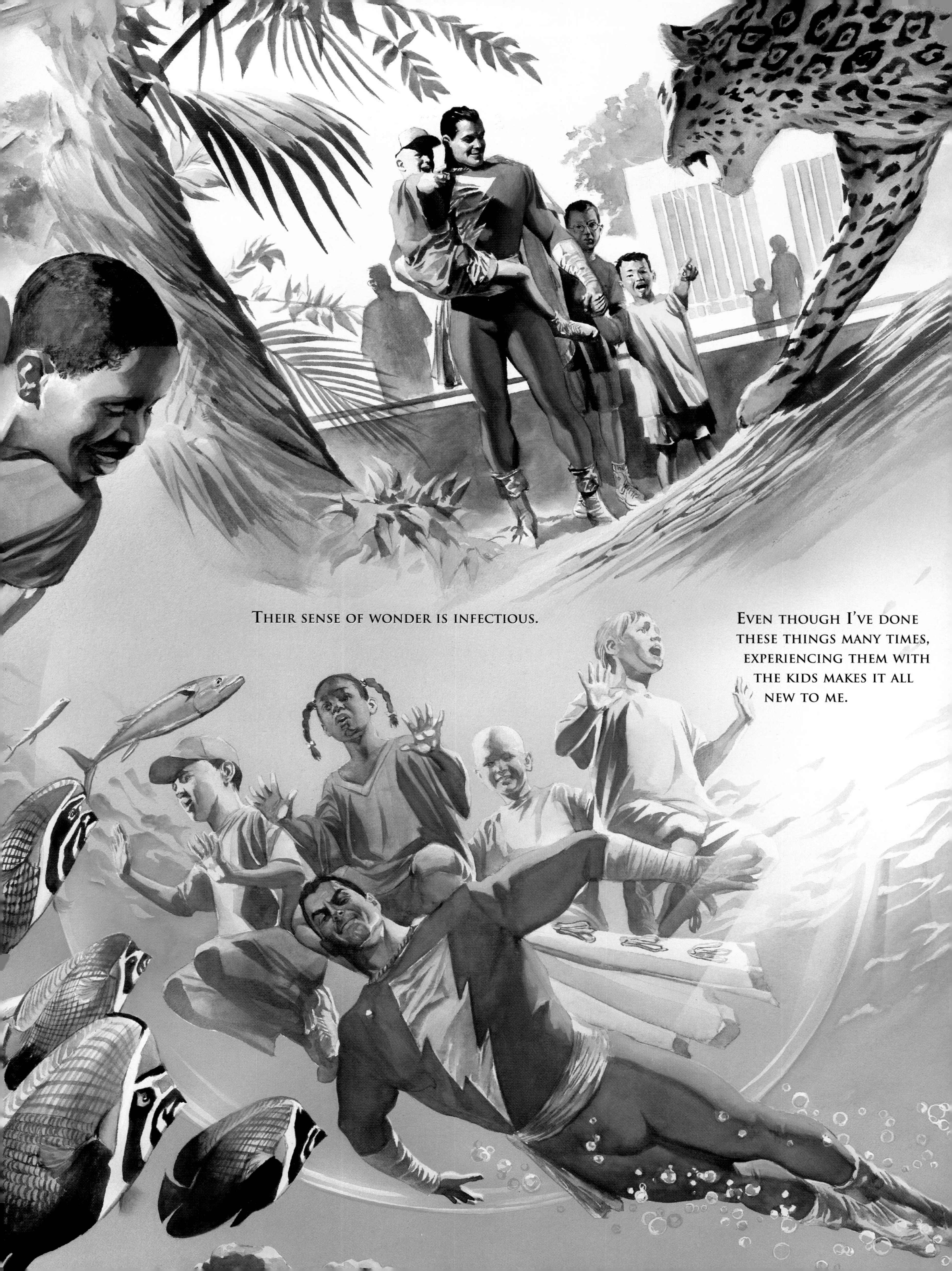
THEIR SENSE OF WONDER IS INFECTIOUS.
EVEN THOUGH I'VE DONE THESE THINGS MANY TIMES, EXPERIENCING THEM WITH THE KIDS MAKES IT ALL NEW TO ME.

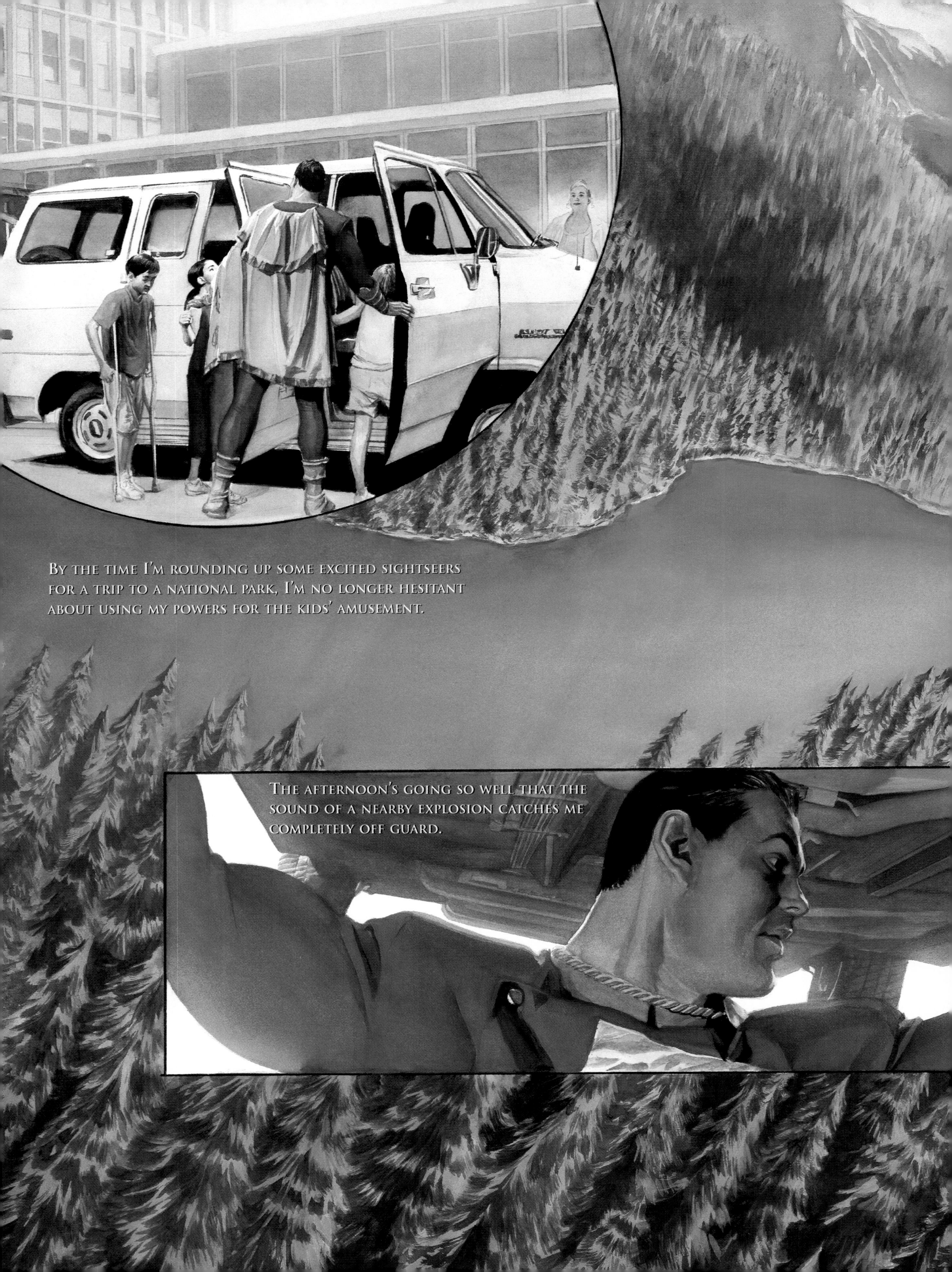
By the time I'm rounding up some excited sightseers for a trip to a national park, I'm no longer hesitant about using my powers for the kids' amusement.
The afternoon's going so well that the sound of a nearby explosion catches me completely off guard.

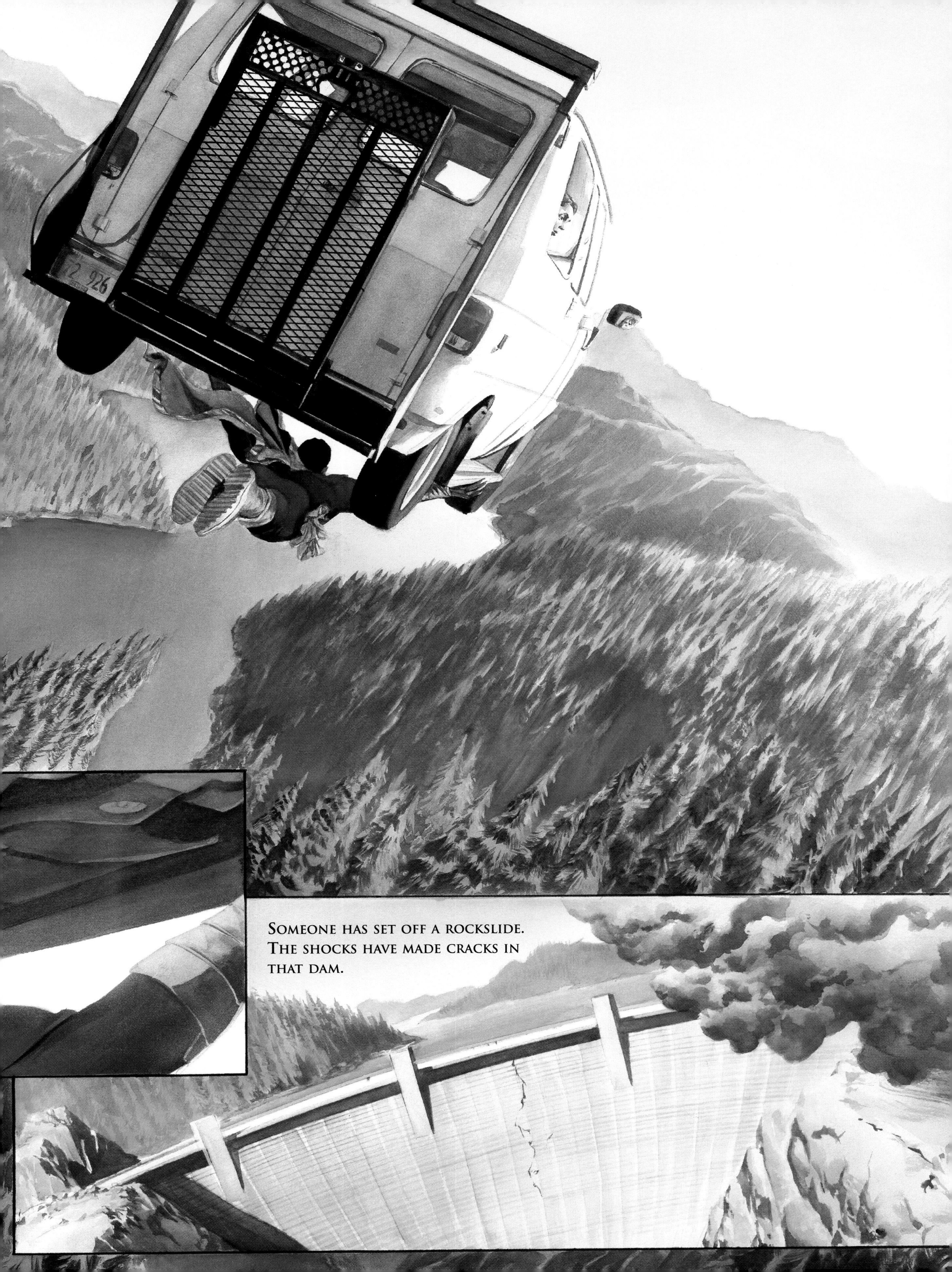
Someone has set off a rockslide. The shocks have made cracks in that dam.

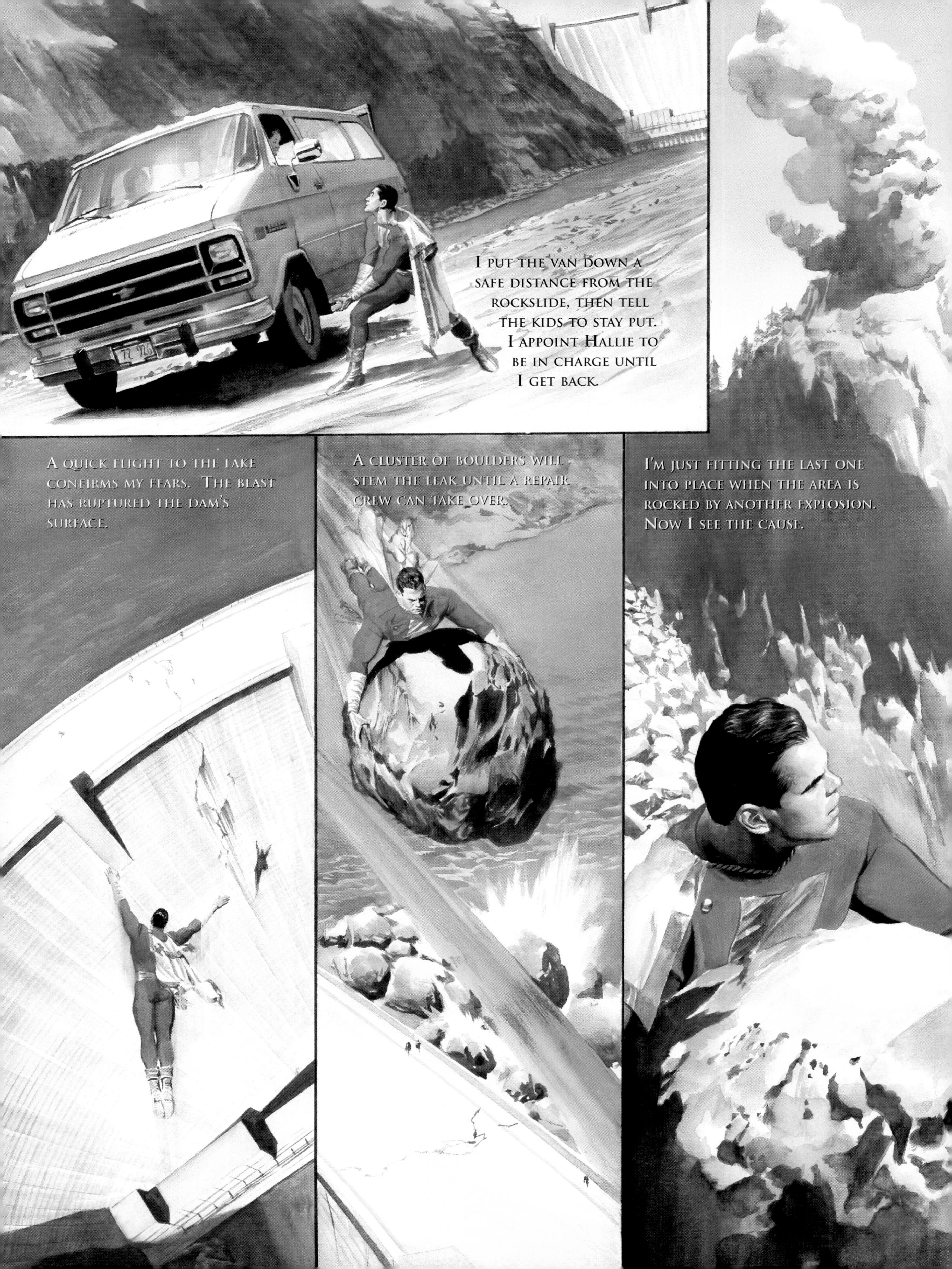
I put the van down a safe distance from the rockslide, then tell the kids to stay put. I appoint Hallie to be in charge until I get back.
A quick flight to the lake confirms my fears. The blast has ruptured the dam's surface.
A cluster of boulders will stem the leak until a repair crew can take over.
I'm just fitting the last one into place when the area is rocked by another explosion. Now I see the cause.

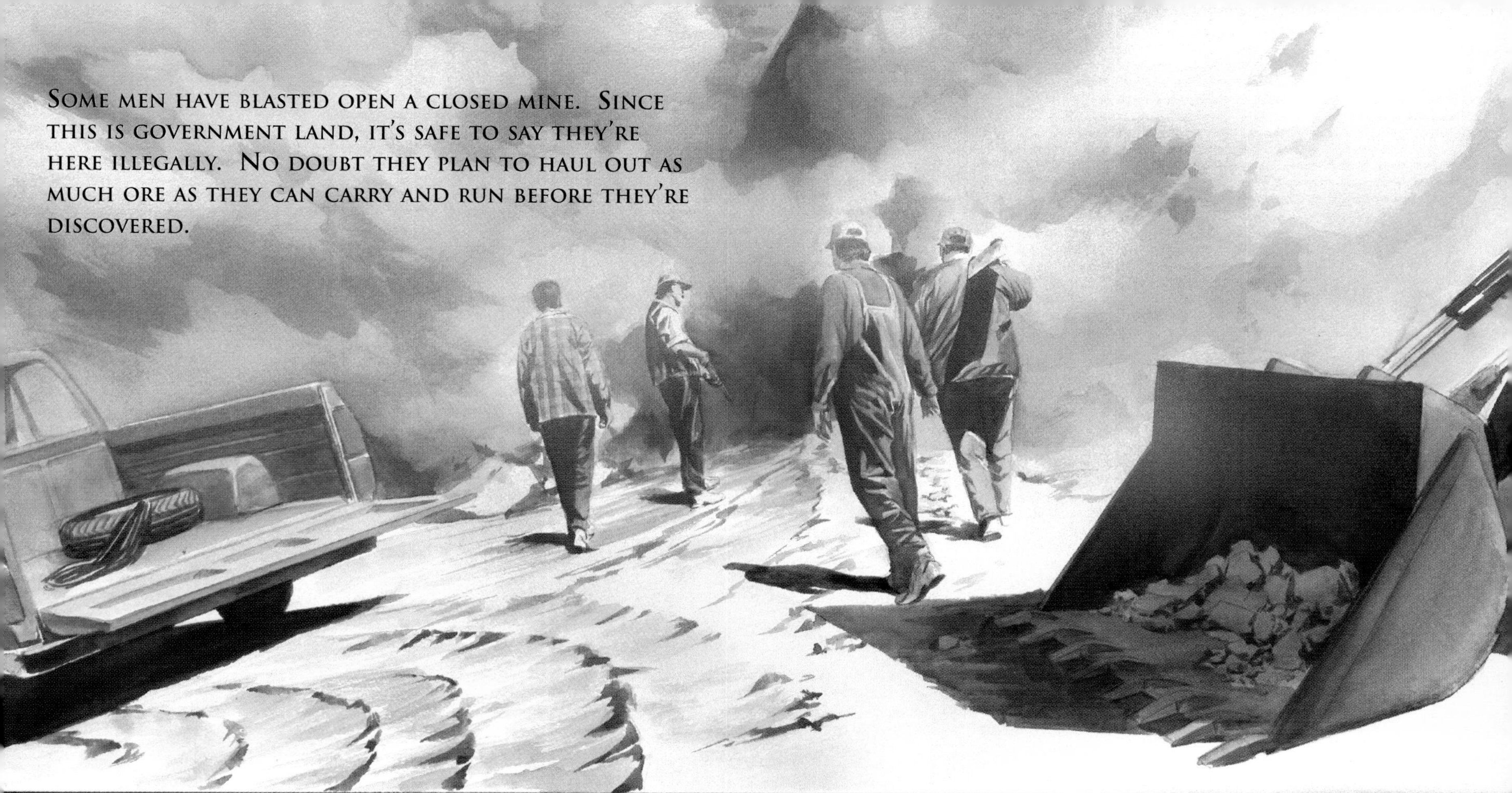
Some men have blasted open a closed mine. Since this is government land, it's safe to say they're here illegally. No doubt they plan to haul out as much ore as they can carry and run before they're discovered.

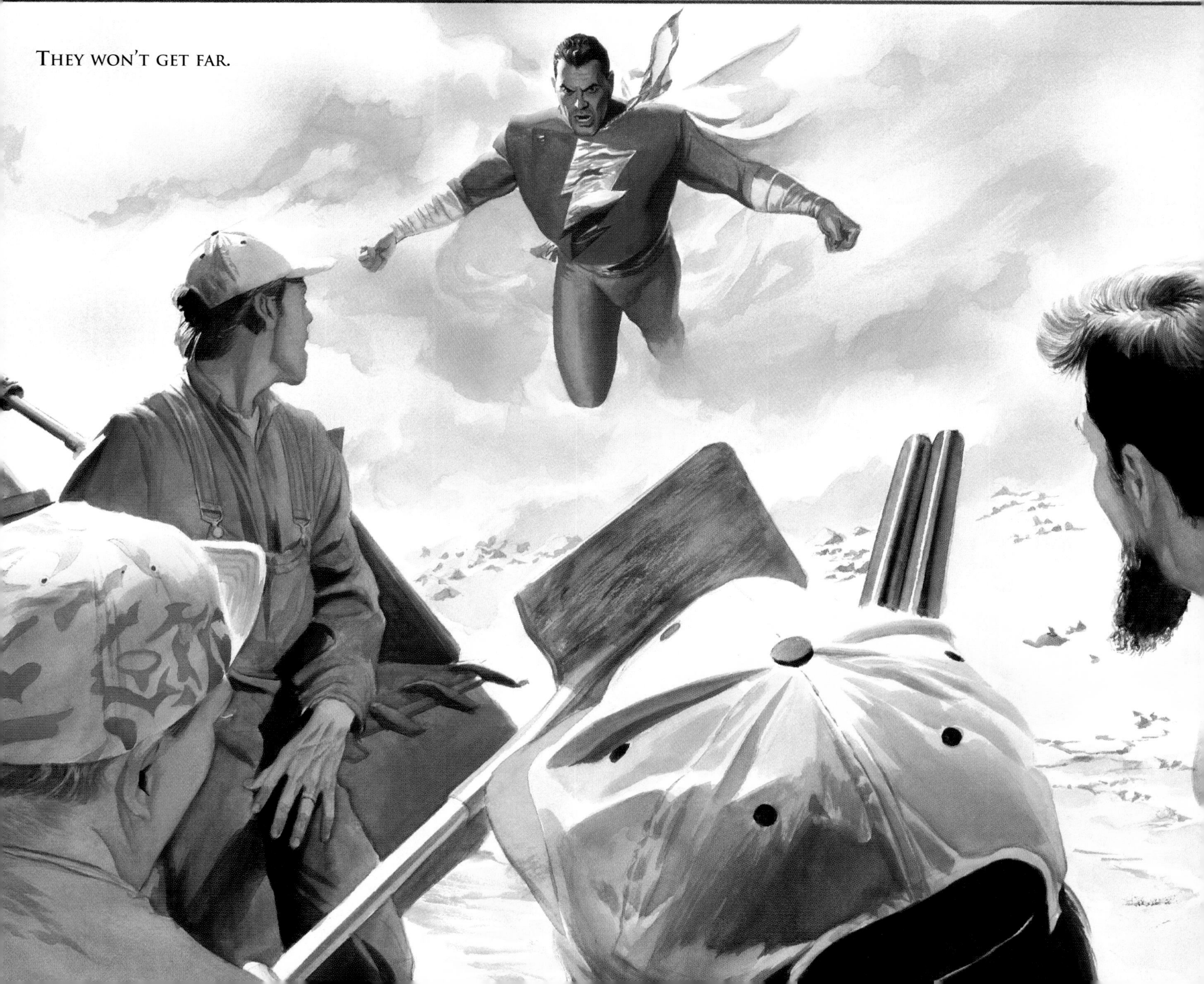
They won't get far.

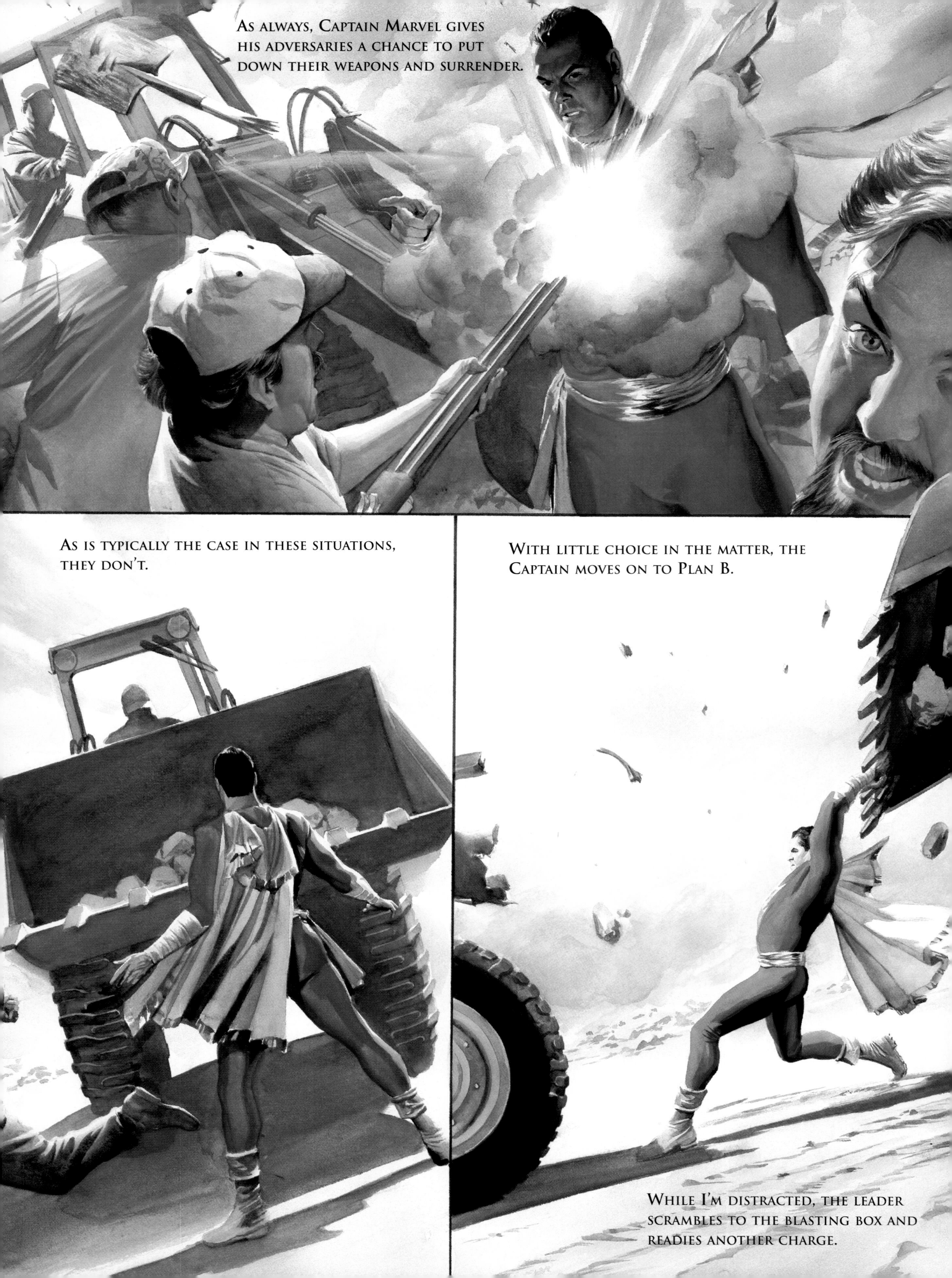
As always, Captain Marvel gives his adversaries a chance to put down their weapons and surrender.
As is typically the case in these situations, they don't.
With little choice in the matter, the Captain moves on to Plan B.
While I'm distracted, the leader scrambles to the blasting box and readies another charge.

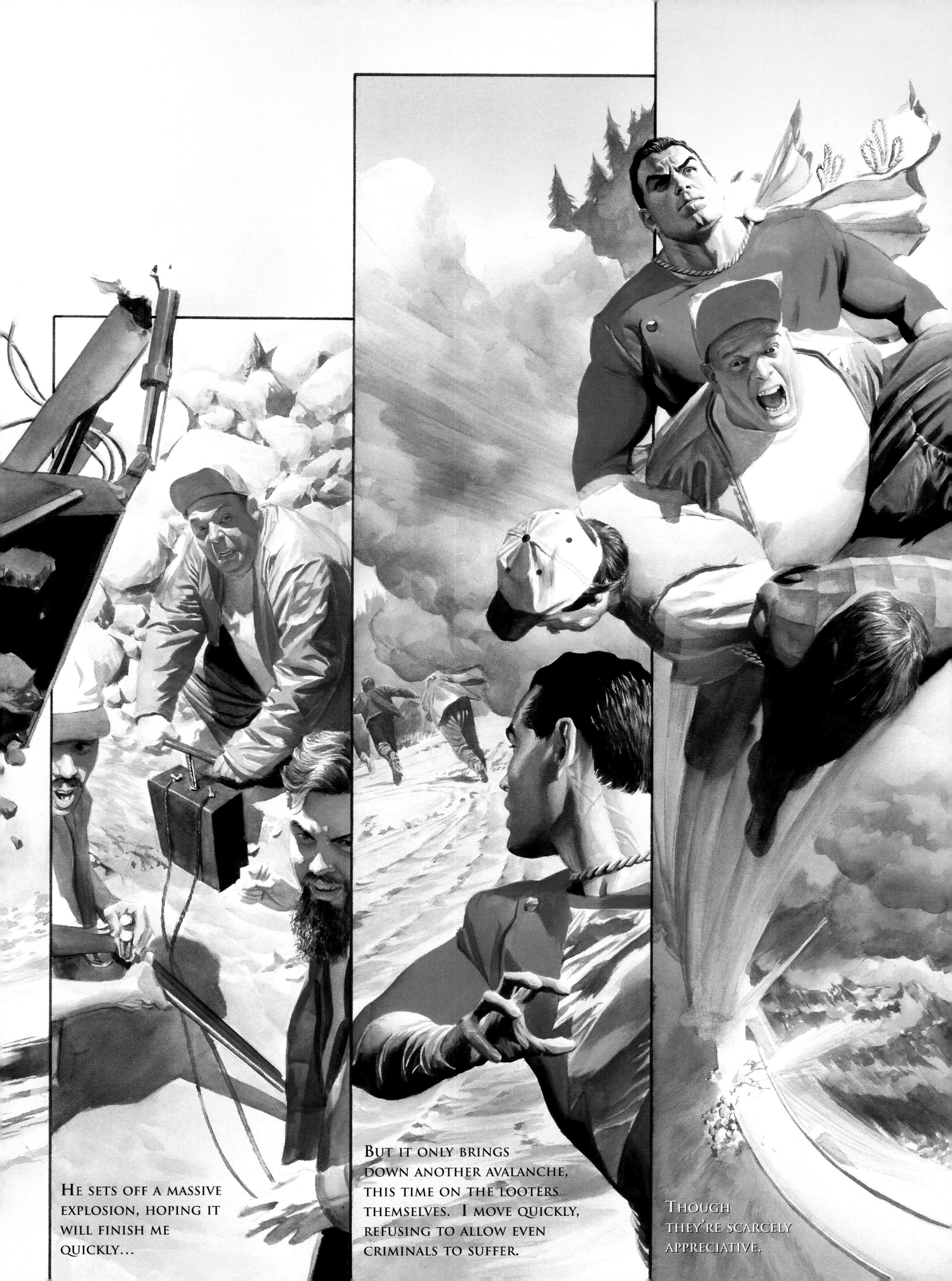
He sets off a massive explosion, hoping it will finish me quickly…
But it only brings down another avalanche, this time on the looters themselves. I move quickly, refusing to allow even criminals to suffer.
Though they're scarcely appreciative.

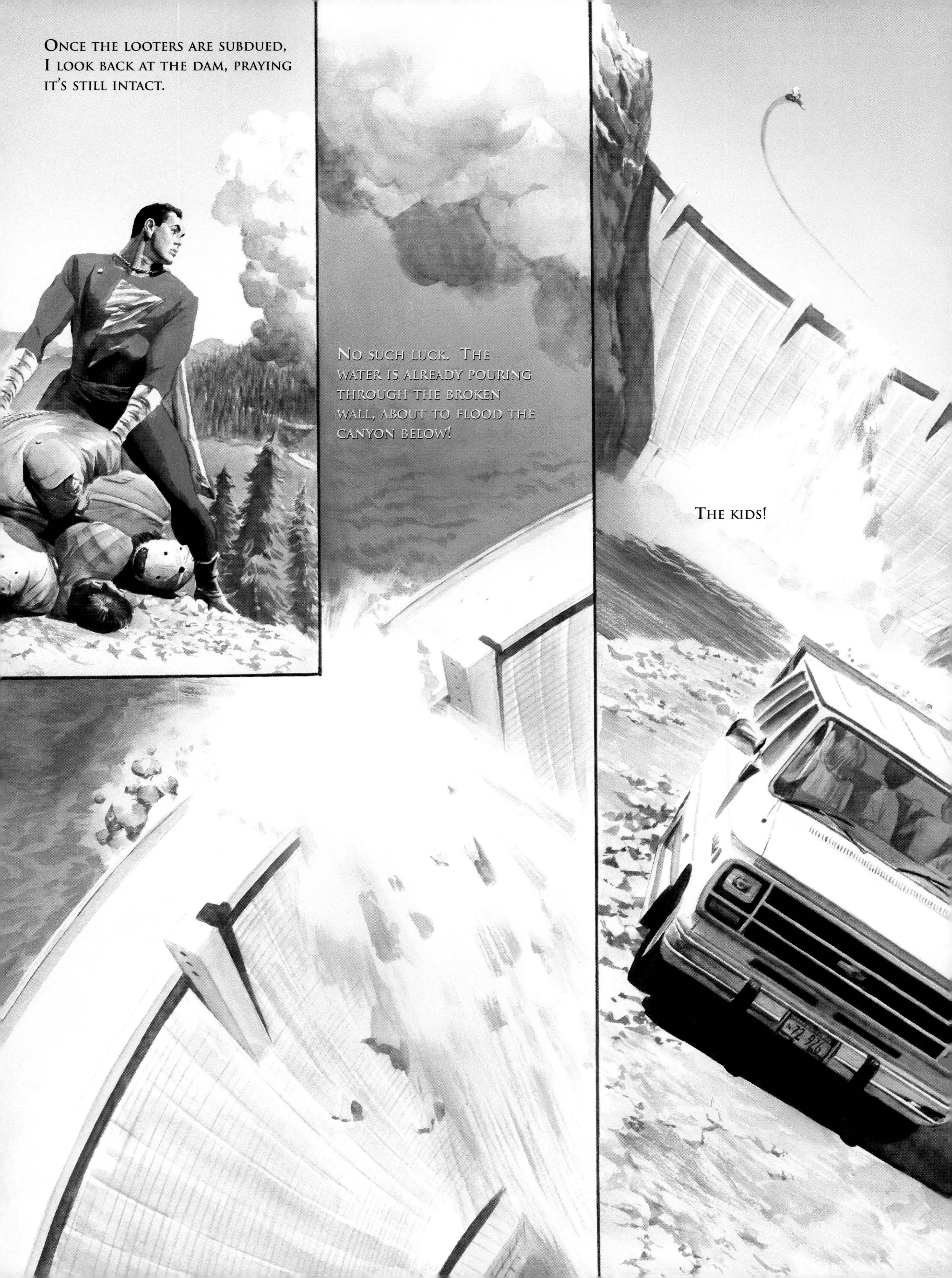
Once the looters are subdued, I look back at the dam, praying it's still intact.
No such luck. The water is already pouring through the broken wall, about to flood the canyon below!
The kids!

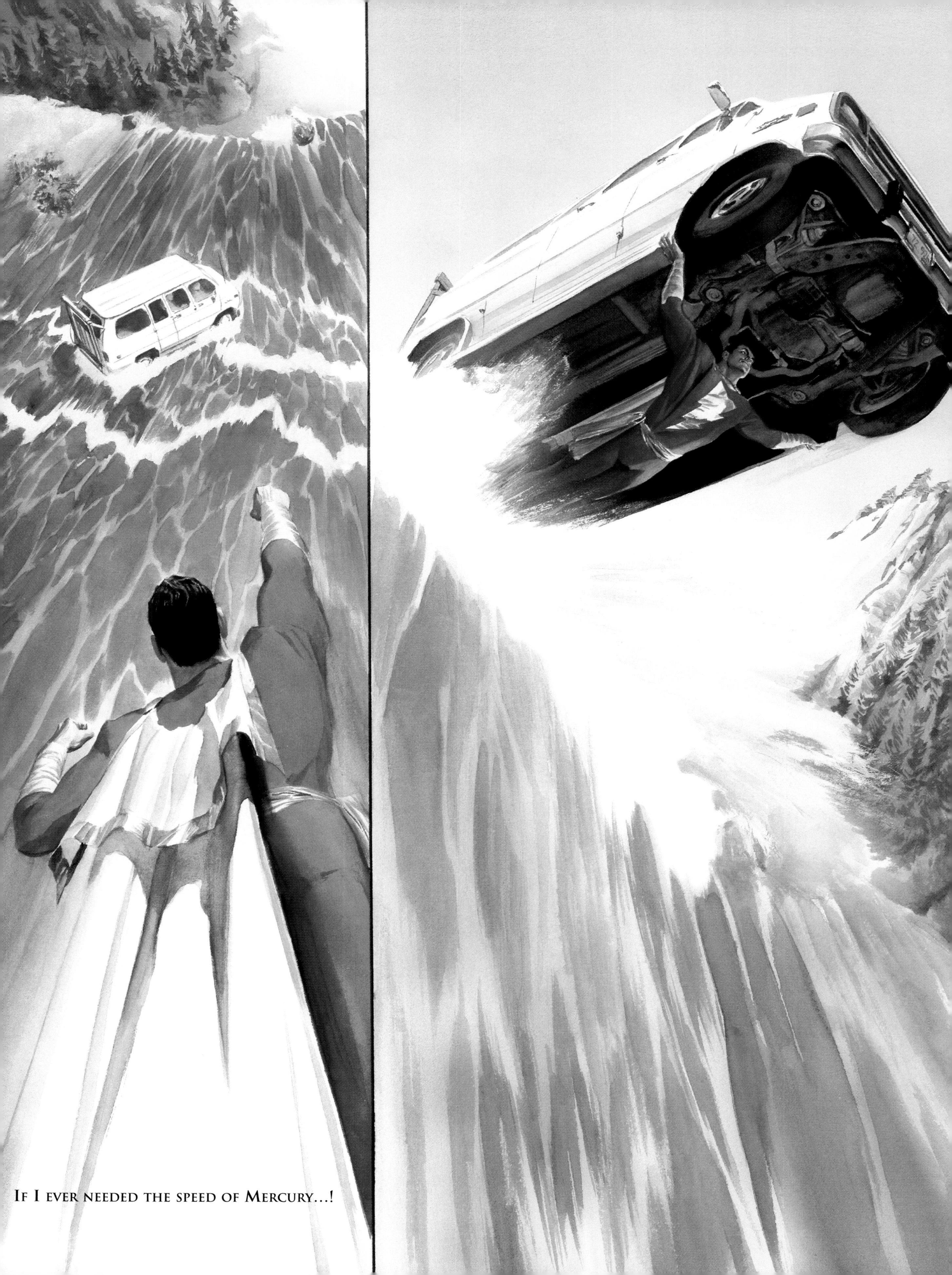
If I ever needed the speed of Mercury...!

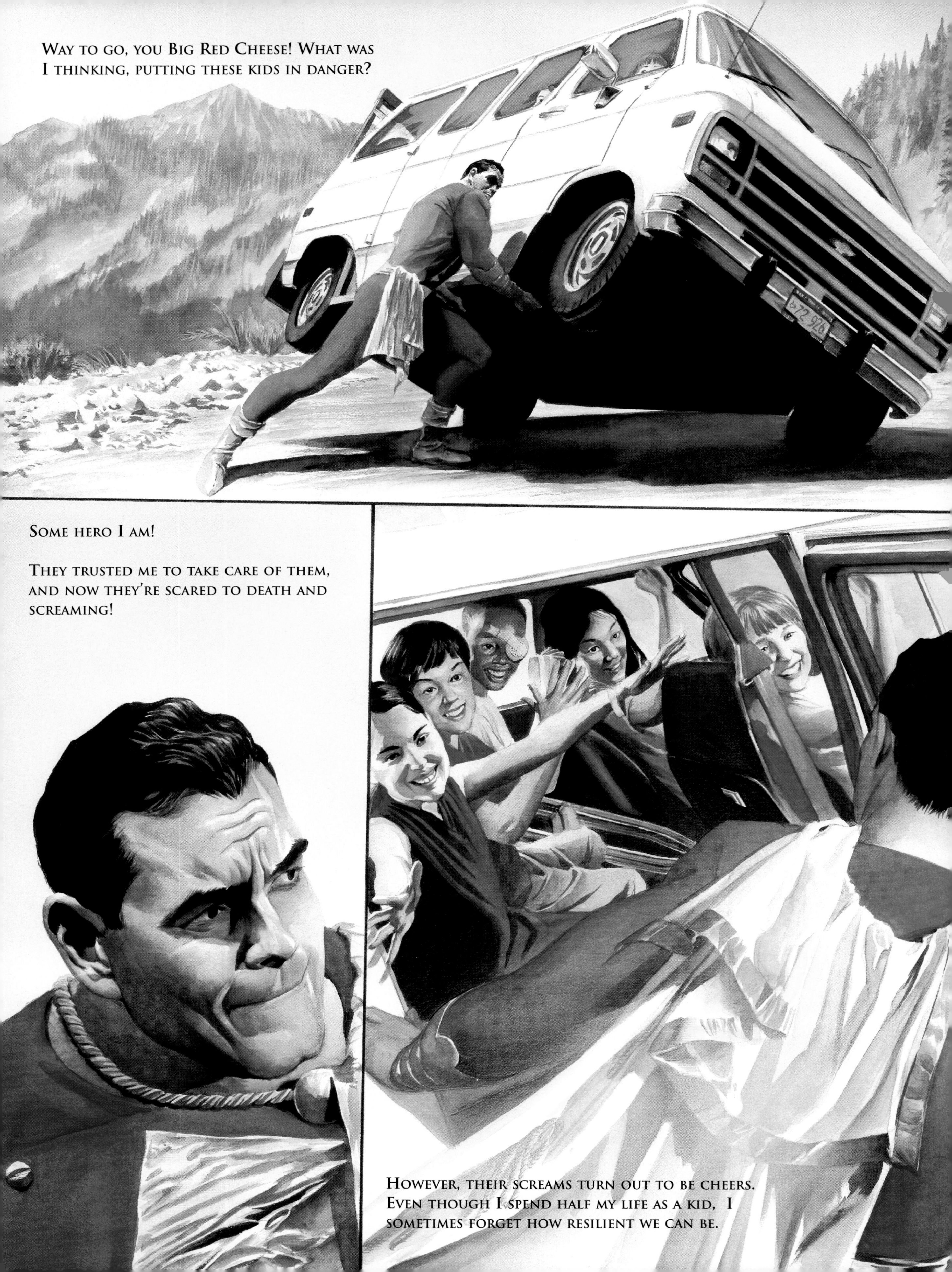
Way to go, you Big Red Cheese! What was I thinking, putting these kids in danger?
Some hero I am!
They trusted me to take care of them, and now they're scared to death and screaming!
However, their screams turn out to be cheers. Even though I spend half my life as a kid, I sometimes forget how resilient we can be.

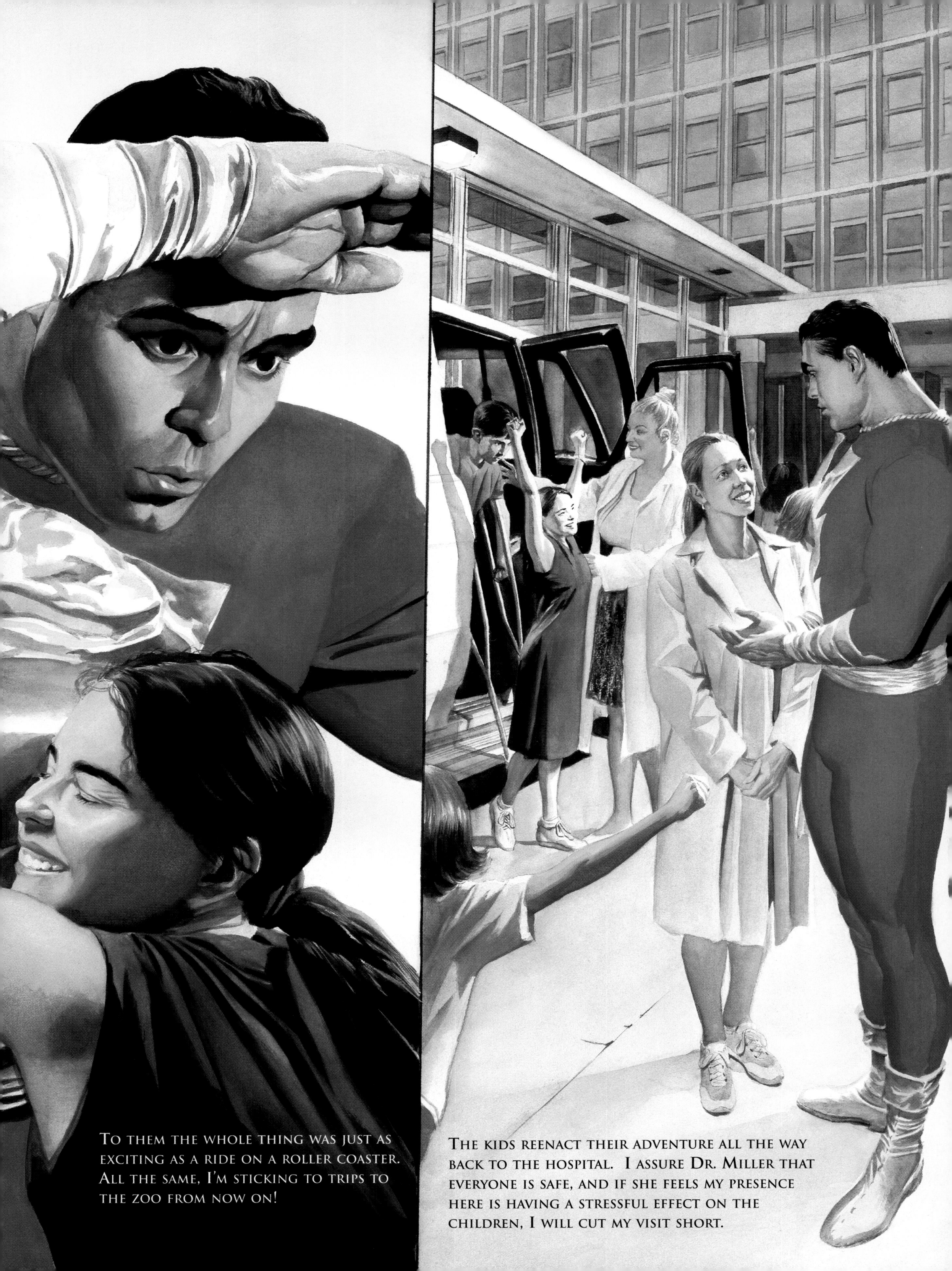
To them the whole thing was just as exciting as a ride on a roller coaster. All the same, I'm sticking to trips to the zoo from now on!
The kids reenact their adventure all the way back to the hospital. I assure Dr. Miller that everyone is safe, and if she feels my presence here is having a stressful effect on the children, I will cut my visit short.

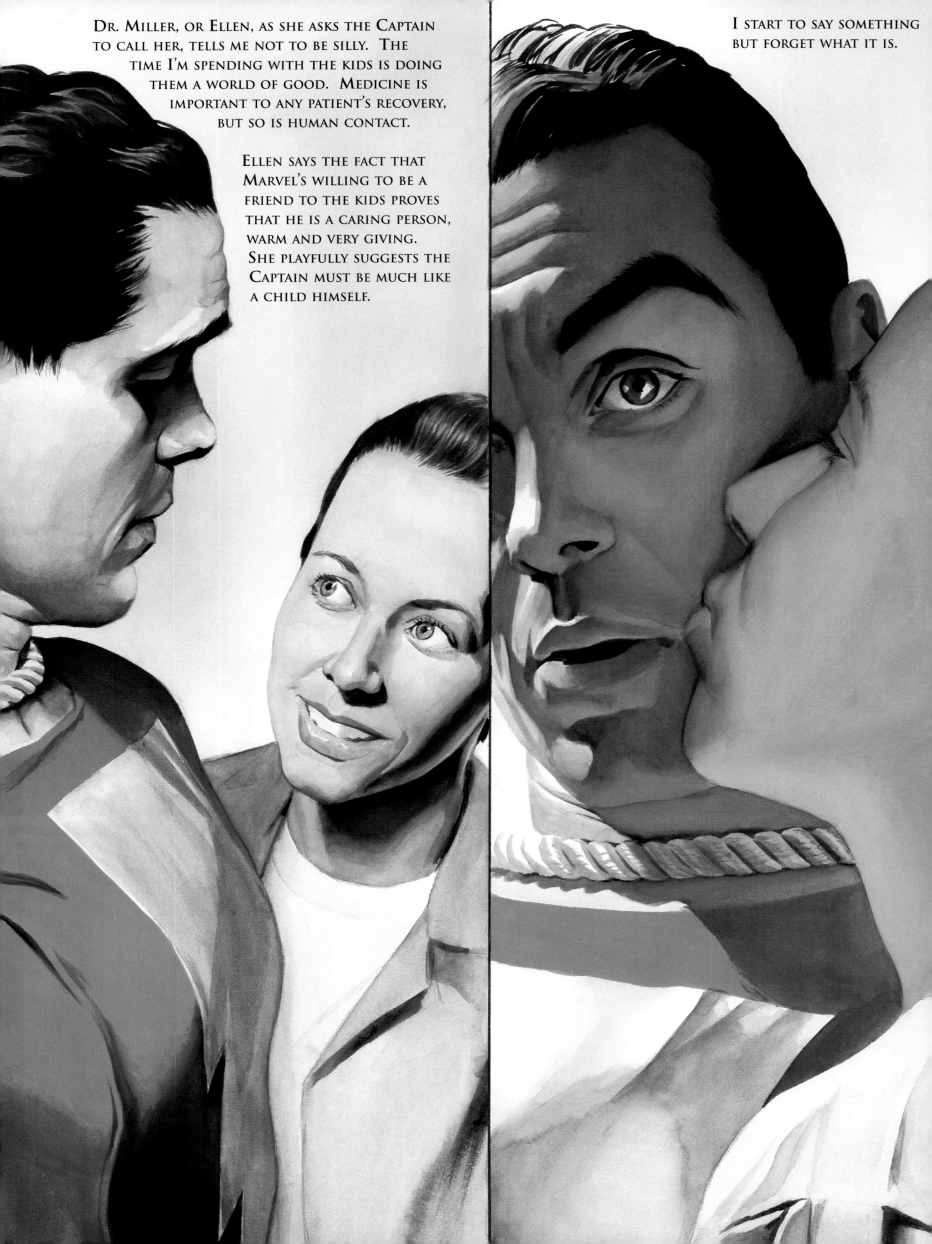

DR. MILLER, OR ELLEN, AS SHE ASKS THE CAPTAIN TO CALL HER, TELLS ME NOT TO BE SILLY. THE TIME I'M SPENDING WITH THE KIDS IS DOING THEM A WORLD OF GOOD. MEDICINE IS IMPORTANT TO ANY PATIENT'S RECOVERY, BUT SO IS HUMAN CONTACT.

ELLEN SAYS THE FACT THAT MARVEL'S WILLING TO BE A FRIEND TO THE KIDS PROVES THAT HE IS A CARING PERSON, WARM AND VERY GIVING. SHE PLAYFULLY SUGGESTS THE CAPTAIN MUST BE MUCH LIKE A CHILD HIMSELF.

I START TO SAY SOMETHING BUT FORGET WHAT IT IS.

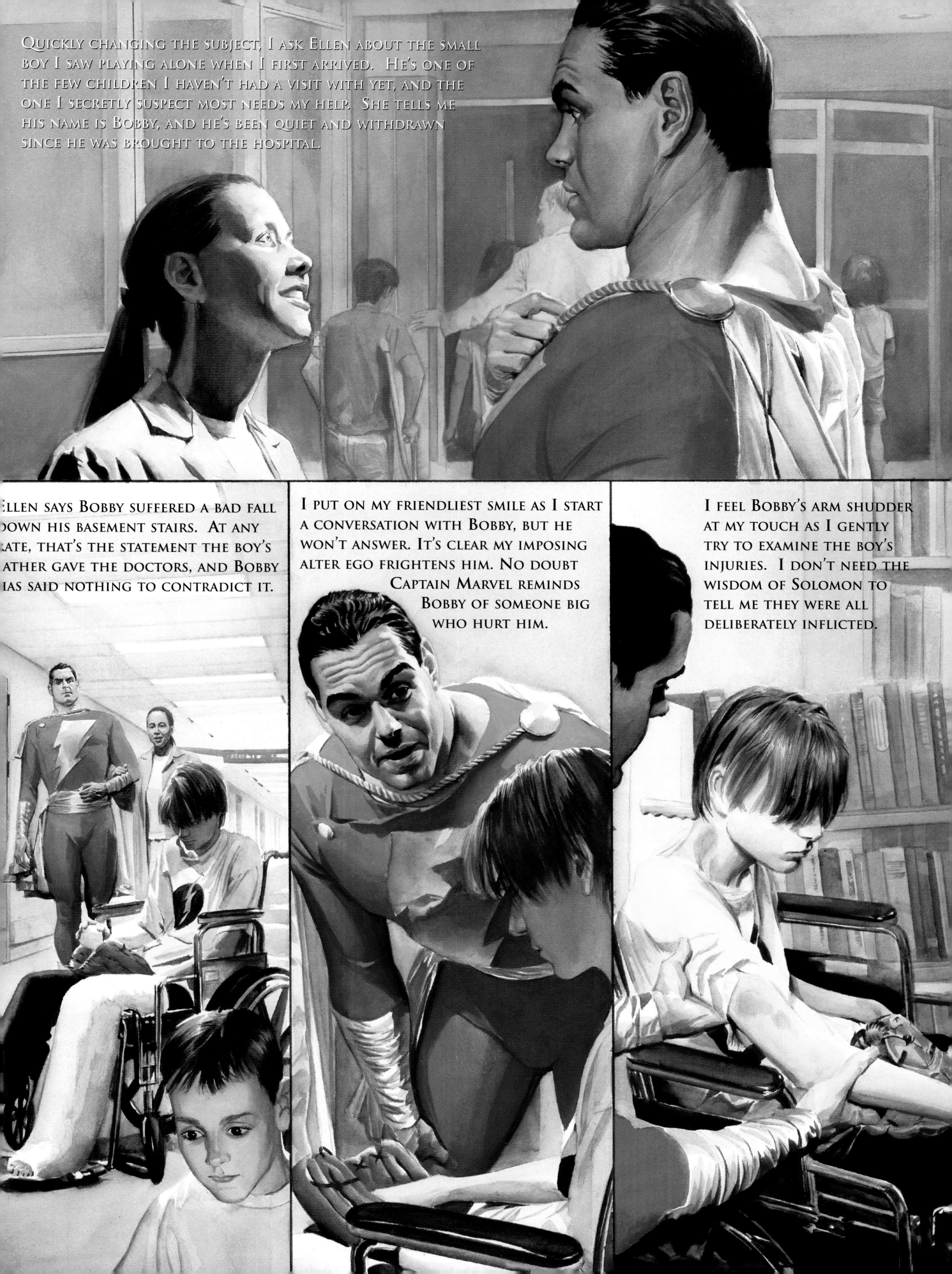
Quickly changing the subject, I ask Ellen about the small boy I saw playing alone when I first arrived. He's one of the few children I haven't had a visit with yet, and the one I secretly suspect most needs my help. She tells me his name is Bobby, and he's been quiet and withdrawn since he was brought to the hospital.
Ellen says Bobby suffered a bad fall down his basement stairs. At any rate, that's the statement the boy's father gave the doctors, and Bobby has said nothing to contradict it.
I put on my friendliest smile as I start a conversation with Bobby, but he won't answer. It's clear my imposing alter ego frightens him. No doubt Captain Marvel reminds Bobby of someone big who hurt him.
I feel Bobby's arm shudder at my touch as I gently try to examine the boy's injuries. I don't need the wisdom of Solomon to tell me they were all deliberately inflicted.

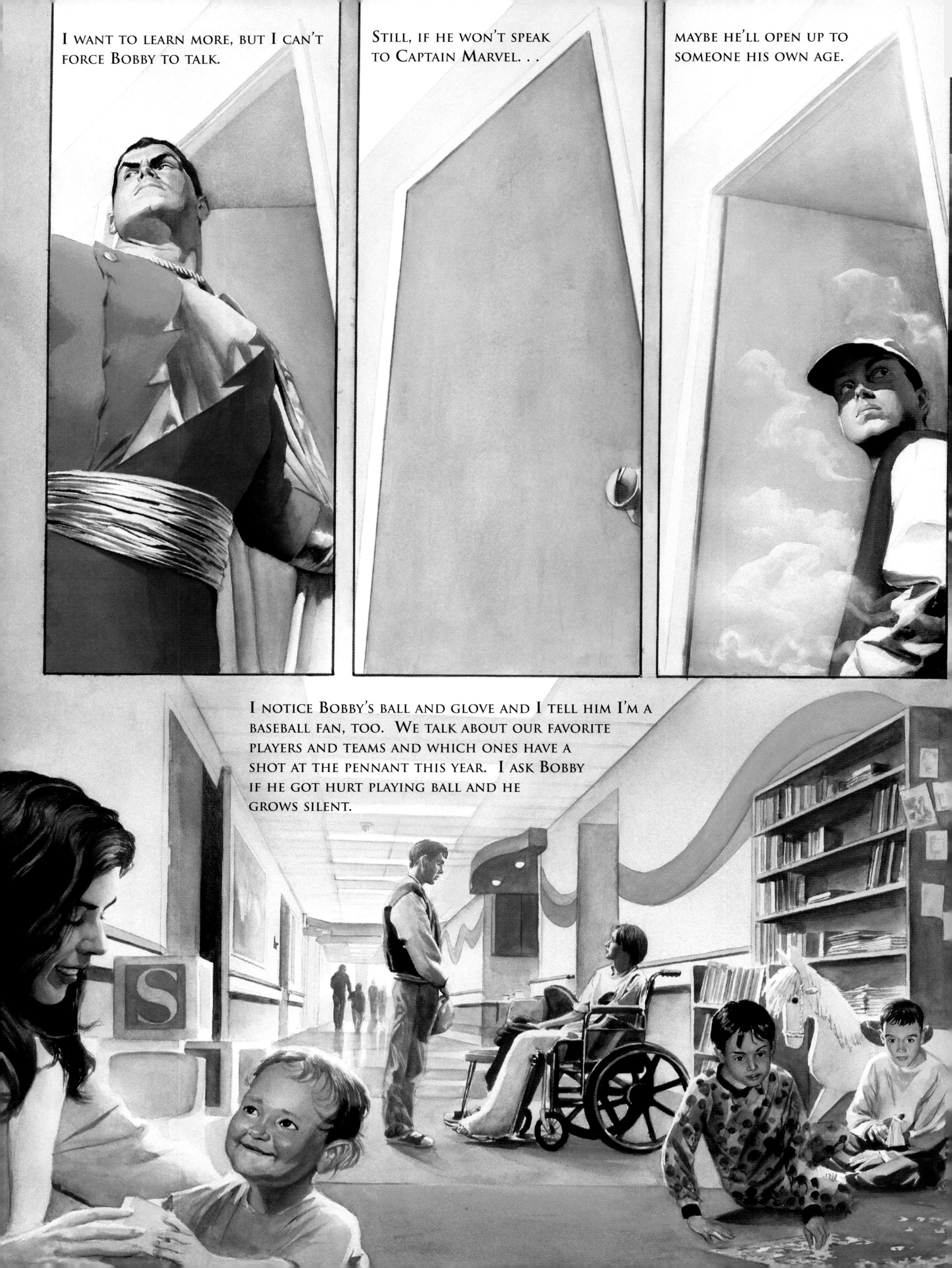
I want to learn more, but I can't force Bobby to talk.
Still, if he won't speak to Captain Marvel. . .
maybe he'll open up to someone his own age.
I notice Bobby's ball and glove and I tell him I'm a baseball fan, too. We talk about our favorite players and teams and which ones have a shot at the pennant this year. I ask Bobby if he got hurt playing ball and he grows silent.

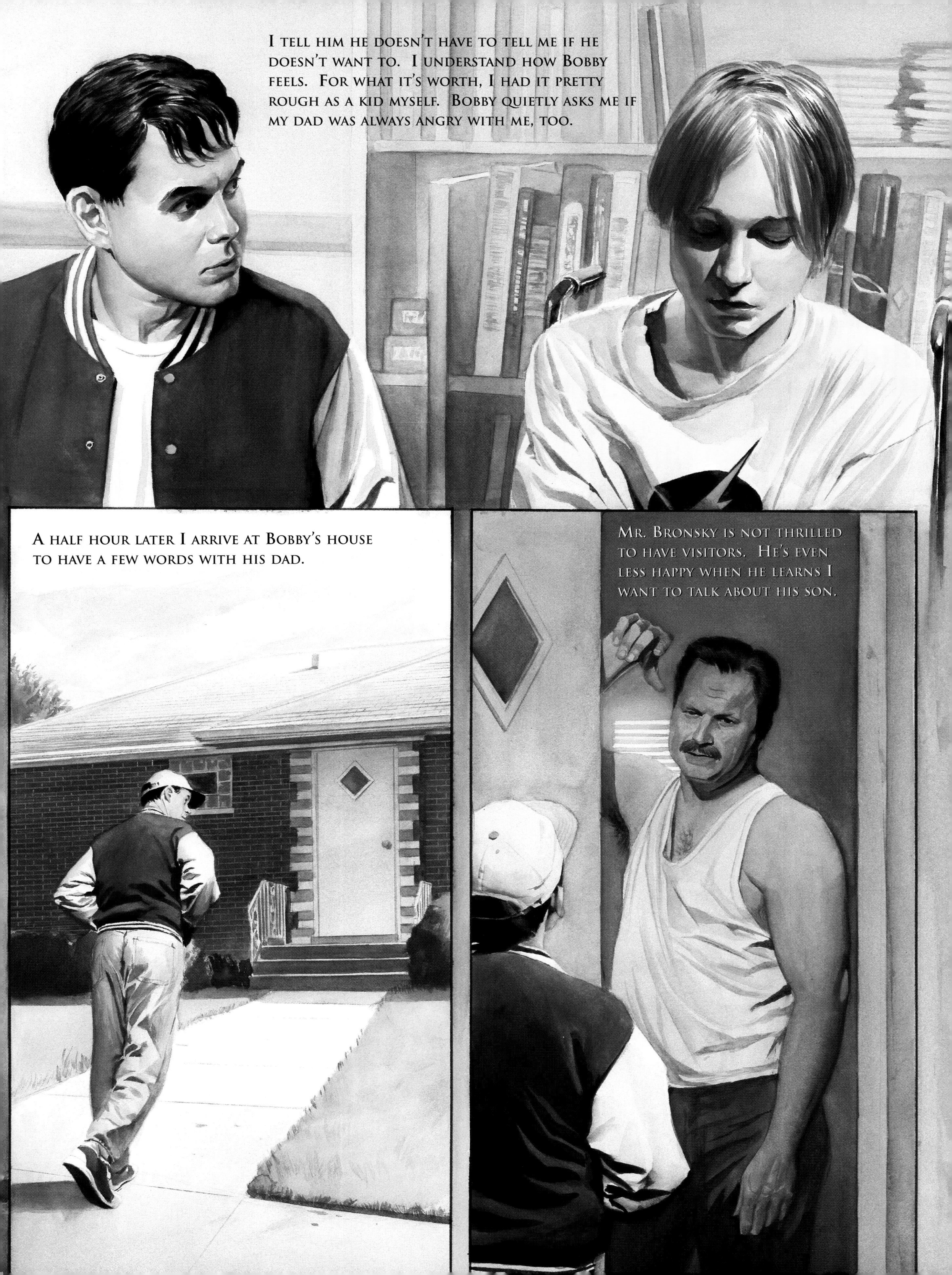
I tell him he doesn't have to tell me if he doesn't want to. I understand how Bobby feels. For what it's worth, I had it pretty rough as a kid myself. Bobby quietly asks me if my dad was always angry with me, too.
A half hour later I arrive at Bobby's house to have a few words with his dad.
Mr. Bronsky is not thrilled to have visitors. He's even less happy when he learns I want to talk about his son.

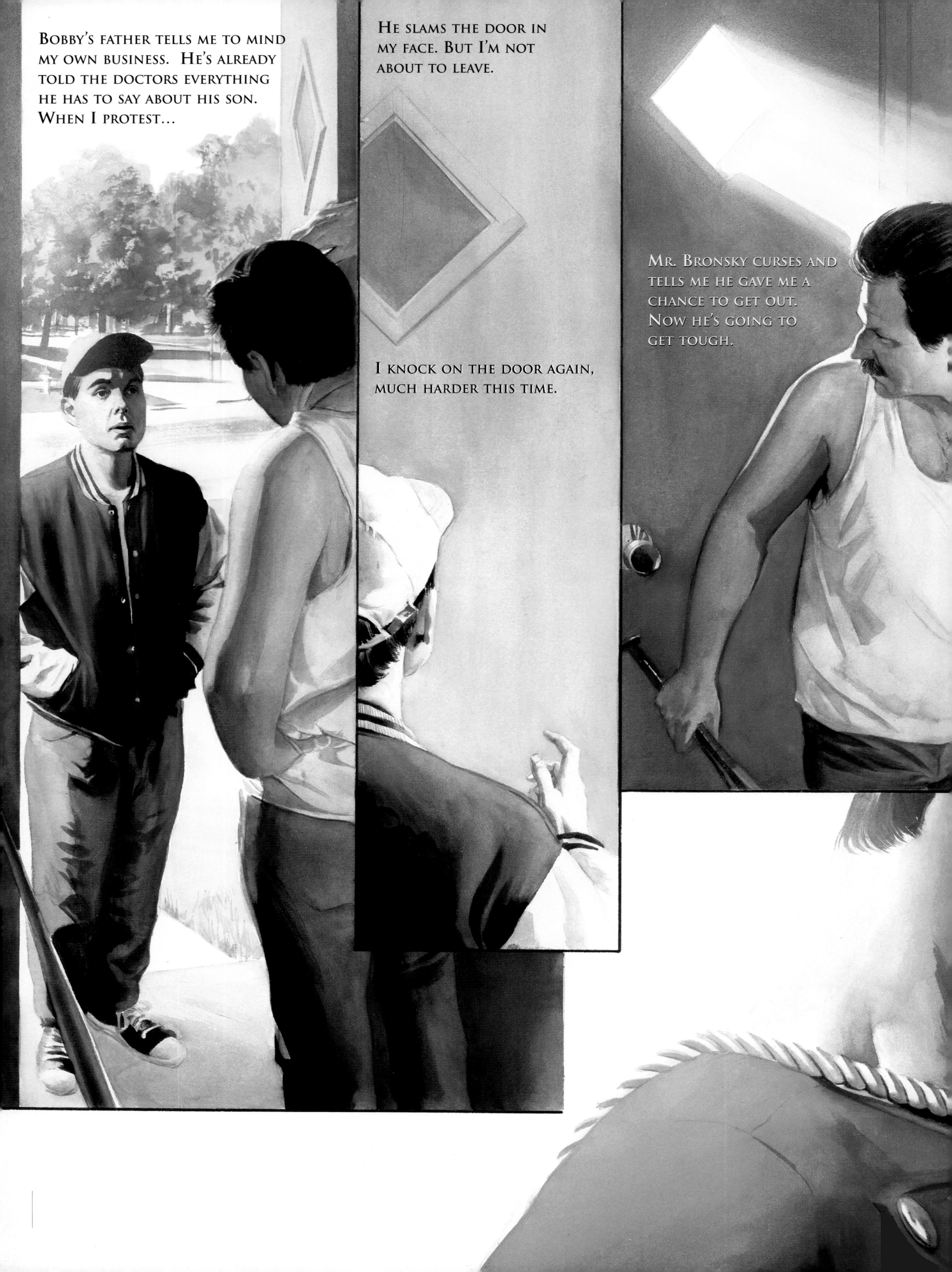

Bobby's father tells me to mind my own business. He's already told the doctors everything he has to say about his son. When I protest...
He slams the door in my face. But I'm not about to leave.
I knock on the door again, much harder this time.
Mr. Bronsky curses and tells me he gave me a chance to get out. Now he's going to get tough.

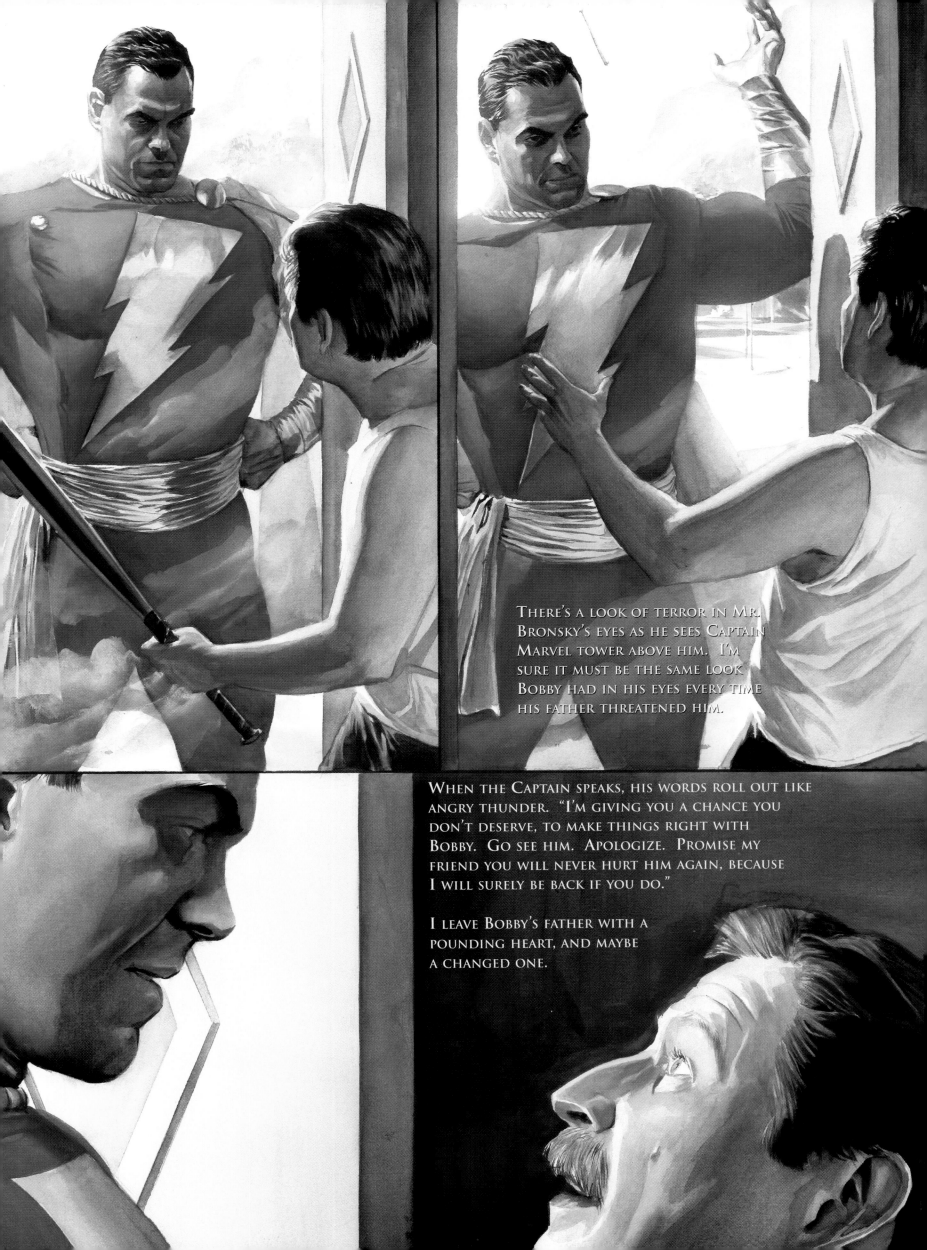

THERE'S A LOOK OF TERROR IN MR. BRONSKY'S EYES AS HE SEES CAPTAIN MARVEL TOWER ABOVE HIM. I'M SURE IT MUST BE THE SAME LOOK BOBBY HAD IN HIS EYES EVERY TIME HIS FATHER THREATENED HIM.

WHEN THE CAPTAIN SPEAKS, HIS WORDS ROLL OUT LIKE ANGRY THUNDER. "I'M GIVING YOU A CHANCE YOU DON'T DESERVE, TO MAKE THINGS RIGHT WITH BOBBY. GO SEE HIM. APOLOGIZE. PROMISE MY FRIEND YOU WILL NEVER HURT HIM AGAIN, BECAUSE I WILL SURELY BE BACK IF YOU DO."

I LEAVE BOBBY'S FATHER WITH A POUNDING HEART, AND MAYBE A CHANGED ONE.

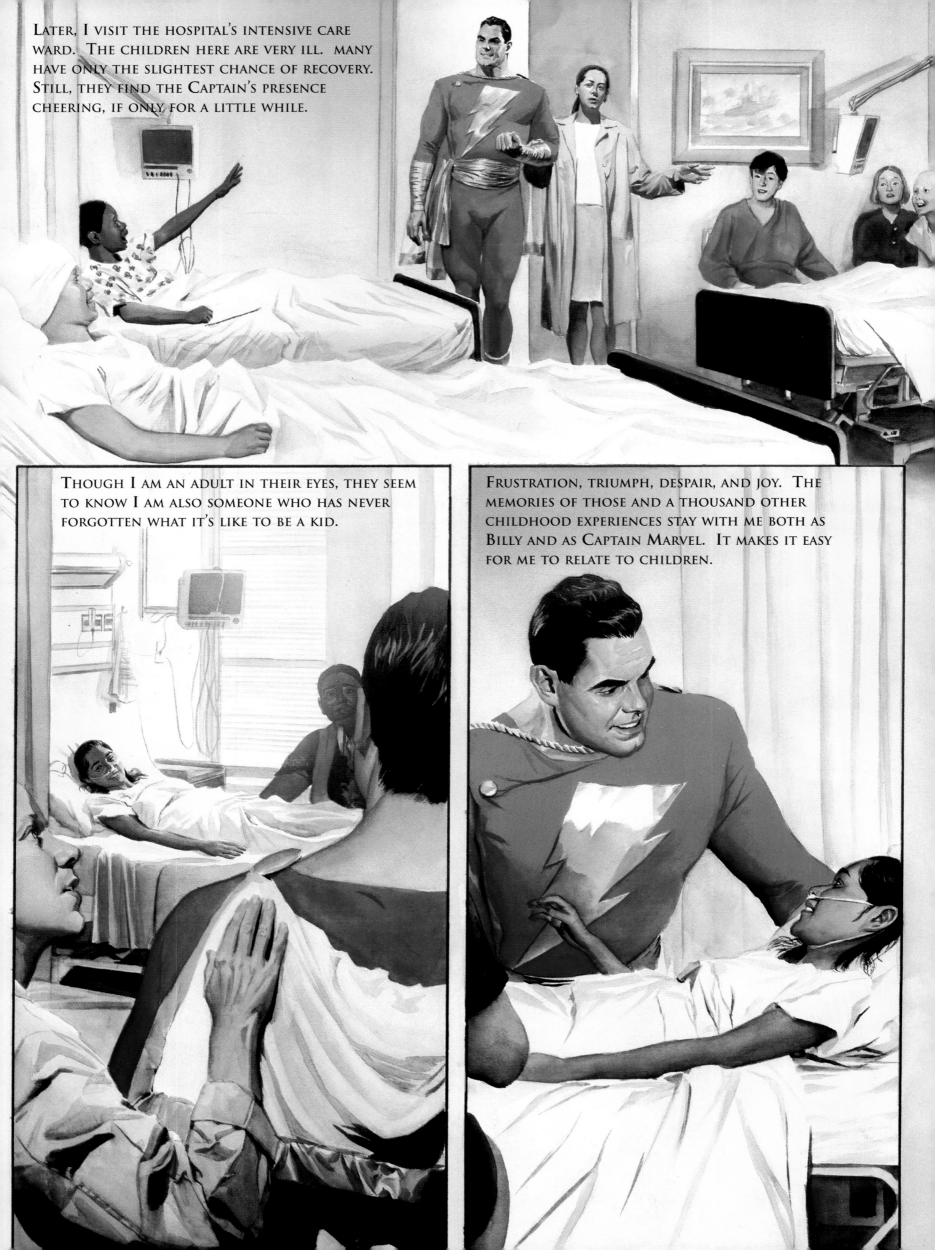

LATER, I VISIT THE HOSPITAL'S INTENSIVE CARE WARD. THE CHILDREN HERE ARE VERY ILL. MANY HAVE ONLY THE SLIGHTEST CHANCE OF RECOVERY. STILL, THEY FIND THE CAPTAIN'S PRESENCE CHEERING, IF ONLY FOR A LITTLE WHILE.

THOUGH I AM AN ADULT IN THEIR EYES, THEY SEEM TO KNOW I AM ALSO SOMEONE WHO HAS NEVER FORGOTTEN WHAT IT'S LIKE TO BE A KID.

FRUSTRATION, TRIUMPH, DESPAIR, AND JOY. THE MEMORIES OF THOSE AND A THOUSAND OTHER CHILDHOOD EXPERIENCES STAY WITH ME BOTH AS BILLY AND AS CAPTAIN MARVEL. IT MAKES IT EASY FOR ME TO RELATE TO CHILDREN.

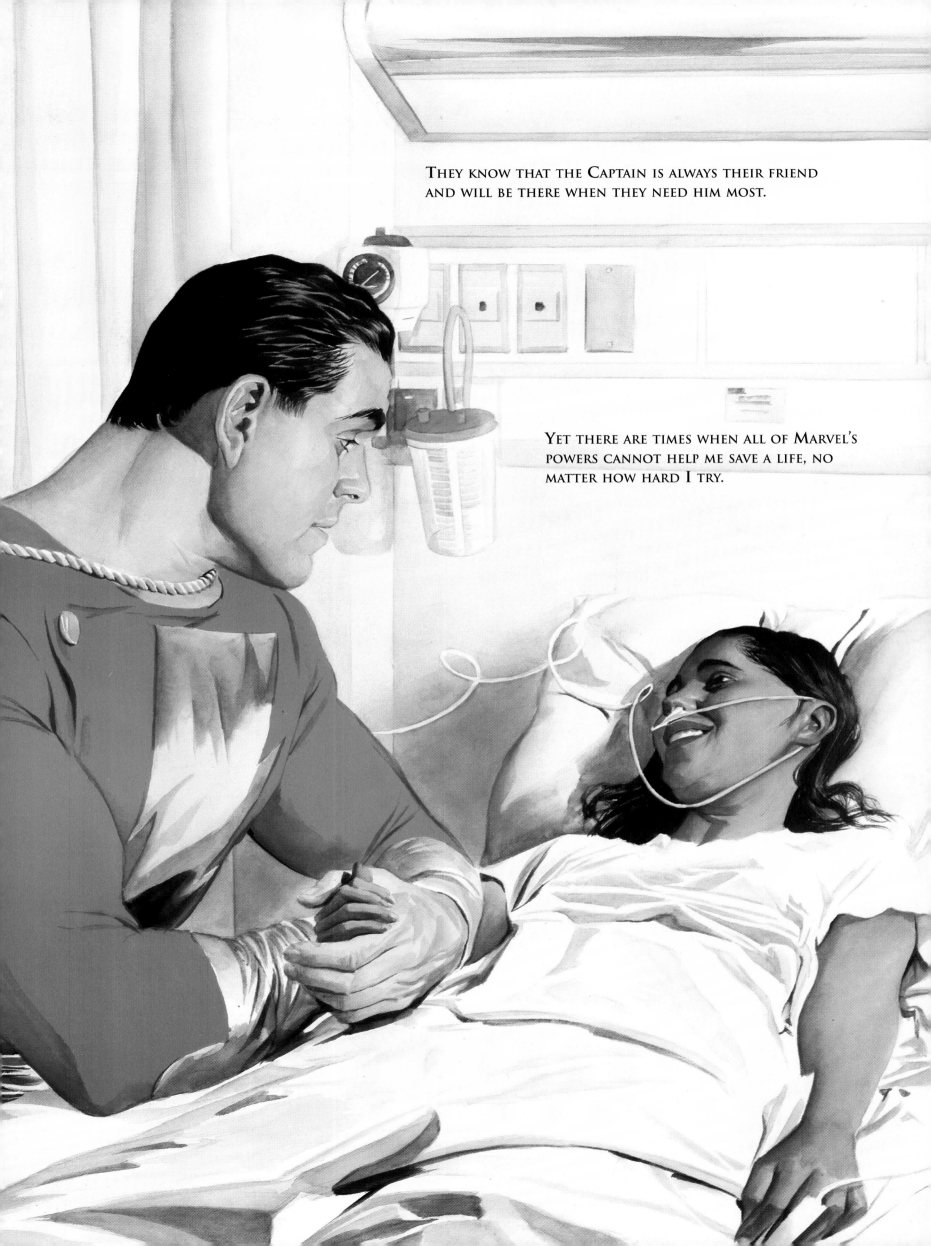

THEY KNOW THAT THE CAPTAIN IS ALWAYS THEIR FRIEND
AND WILL BE THERE WHEN THEY NEED HIM MOST.

YET THERE ARE TIMES WHEN ALL OF MARVEL'S
POWERS CANNOT HELP ME SAVE A LIFE, NO
MATTER HOW HARD I TRY.

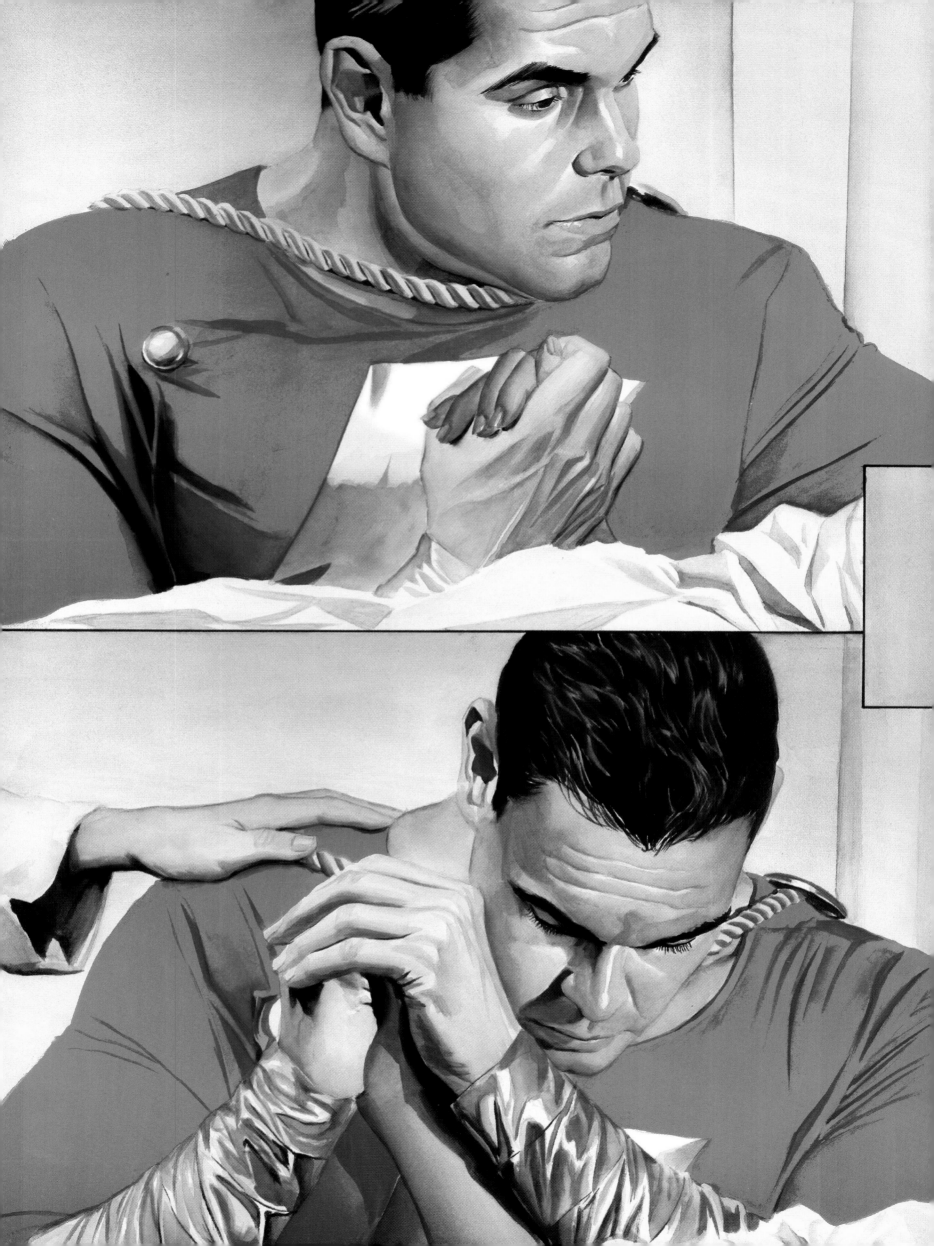

All I have to offer Tanita is a friendly smile, a gentle hand, and a few words of comfort. In my mind that's not nearly enough, but it has made her very happy.

It has given her a reason to smile, a moment of relief from her fear and pain.

And in that moment, she slips away.

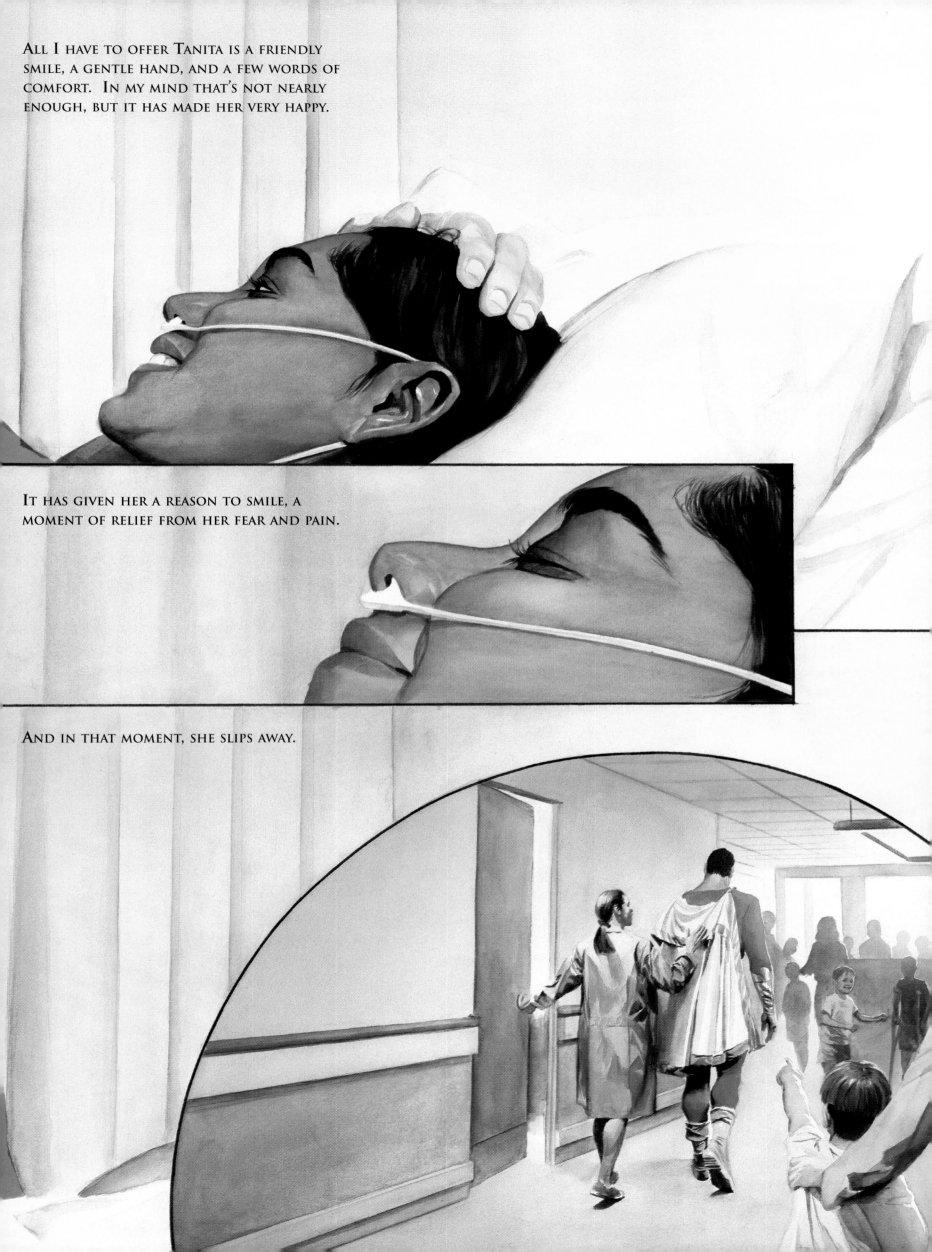

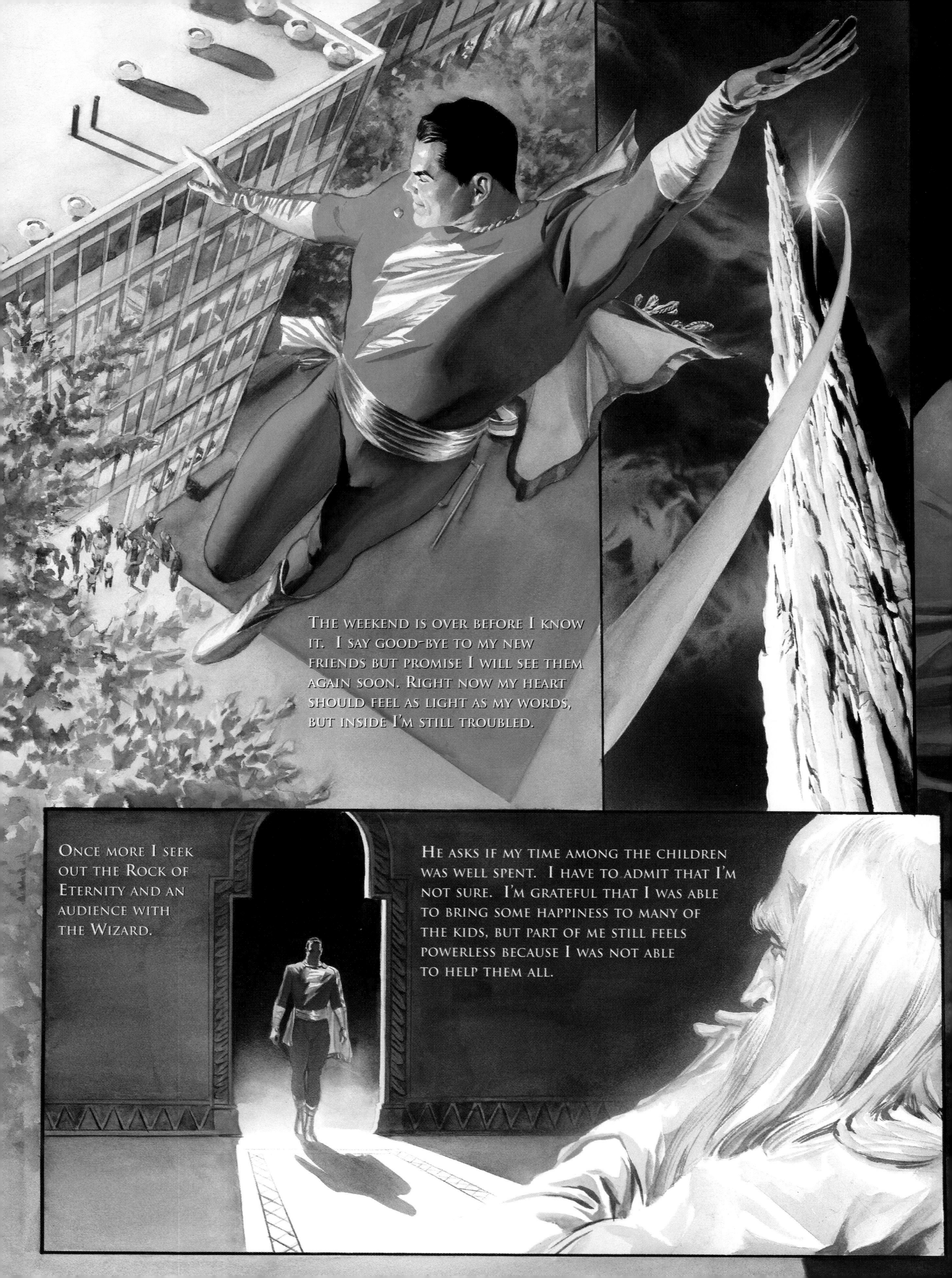
The weekend is over before I know it. I say good-bye to my new friends but promise I will see them again soon. Right now my heart should feel as light as my words, but inside I'm still troubled.
Once more I seek out the Rock of Eternity and an audience with the Wizard.
He asks if my time among the children was well spent. I have to admit that I'm not sure. I'm grateful that I was able to bring some happiness to many of the kids, but part of me still feels powerless because I was not able to help them all.

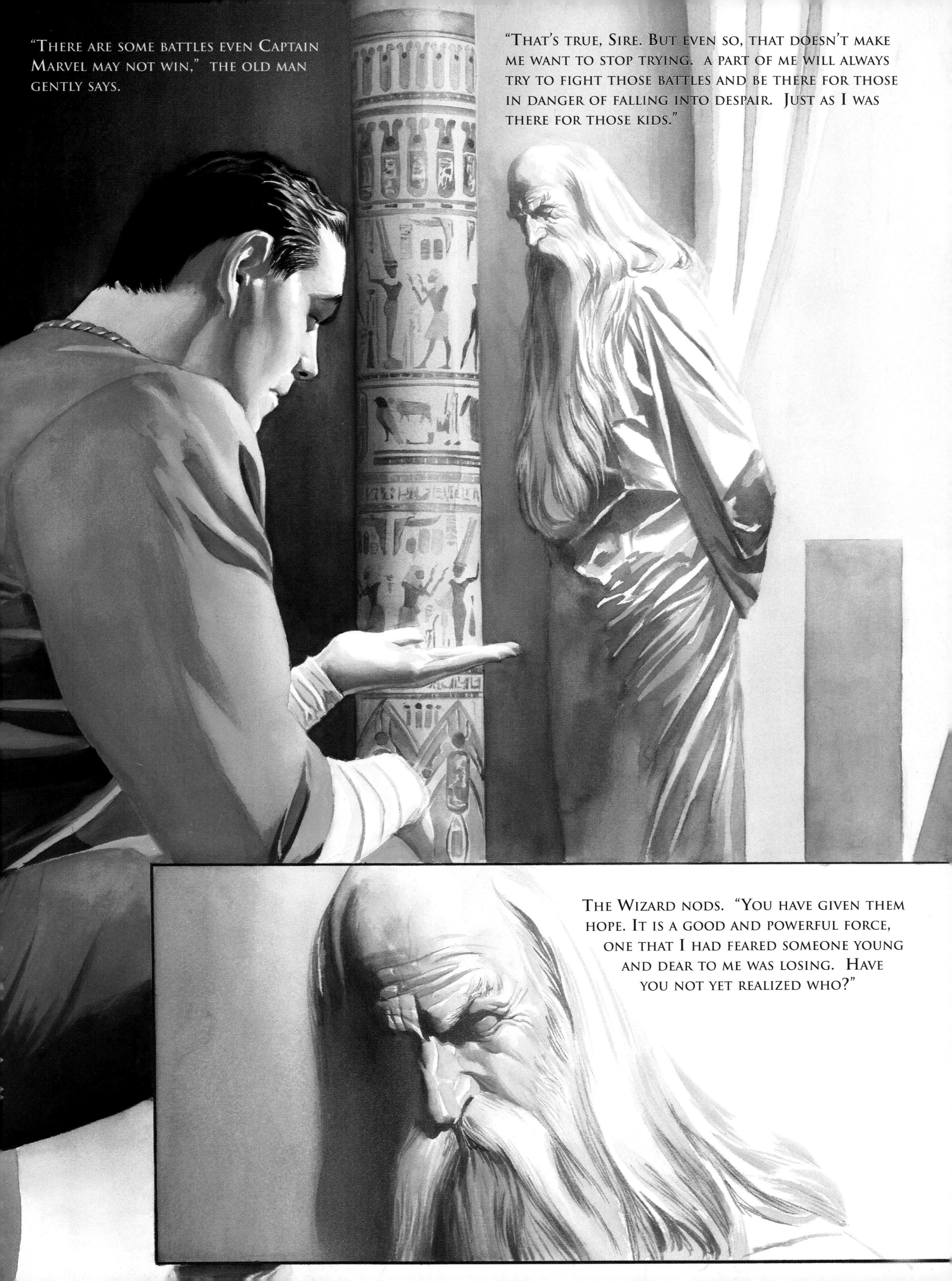
"There are some battles even Captain Marvel may not win," the old man gently says.
"That's true, Sire. But even so, that doesn't make me want to stop trying. A part of me will always try to fight those battles and be there for those in danger of falling into despair. Just as I was there for those kids."
The Wizard nods. "You have given them hope. It is a good and powerful force, one that I had feared someone young and dear to me was losing. Have you not yet realized who?"

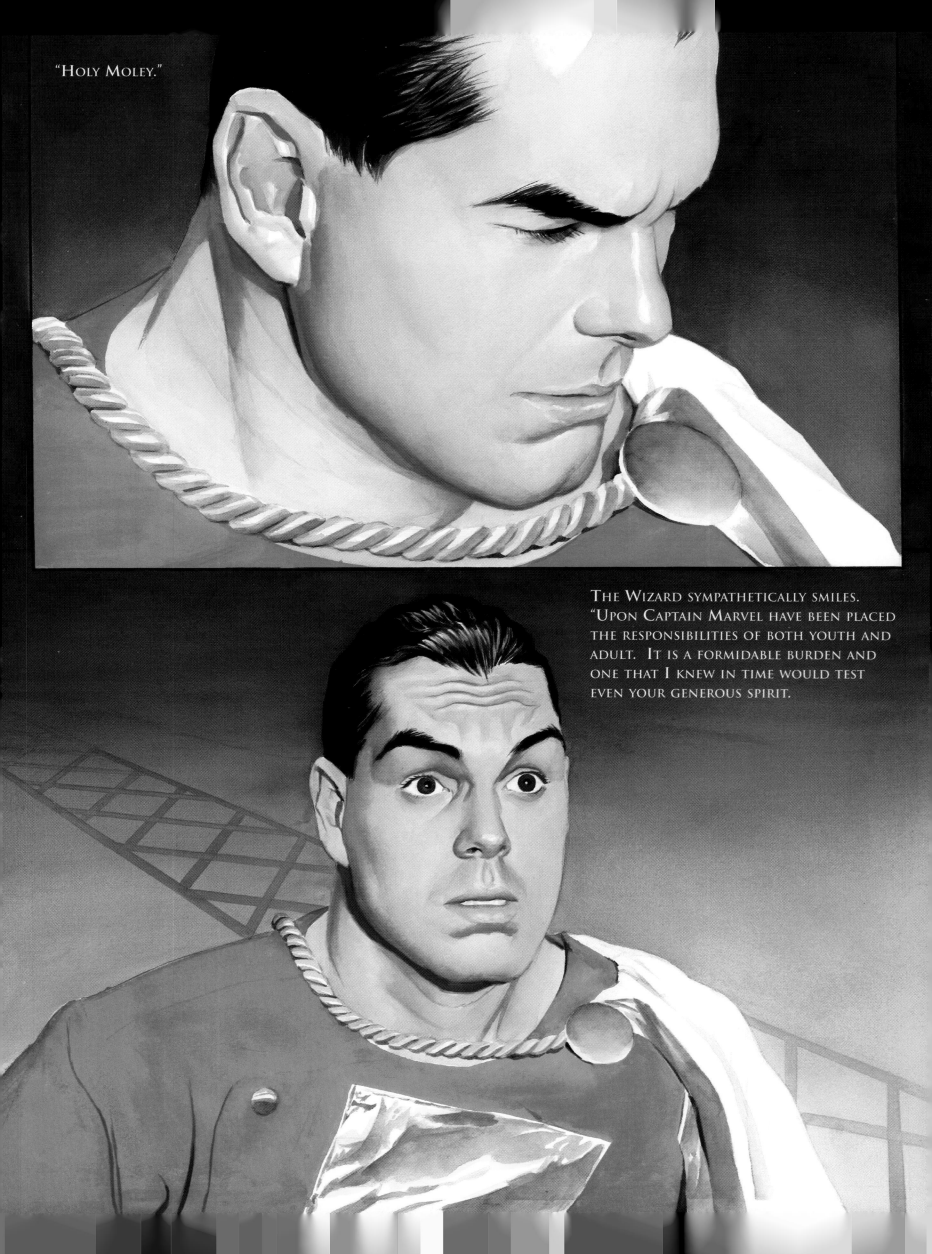

"HOLY MOLEY."

THE WIZARD SYMPATHETICALLY SMILES. "UPON CAPTAIN MARVEL HAVE BEEN PLACED THE RESPONSIBILITIES OF BOTH YOUTH AND ADULT. IT IS A FORMIDABLE BURDEN AND ONE THAT I KNEW IN TIME WOULD TEST EVEN YOUR GENEROUS SPIRIT.

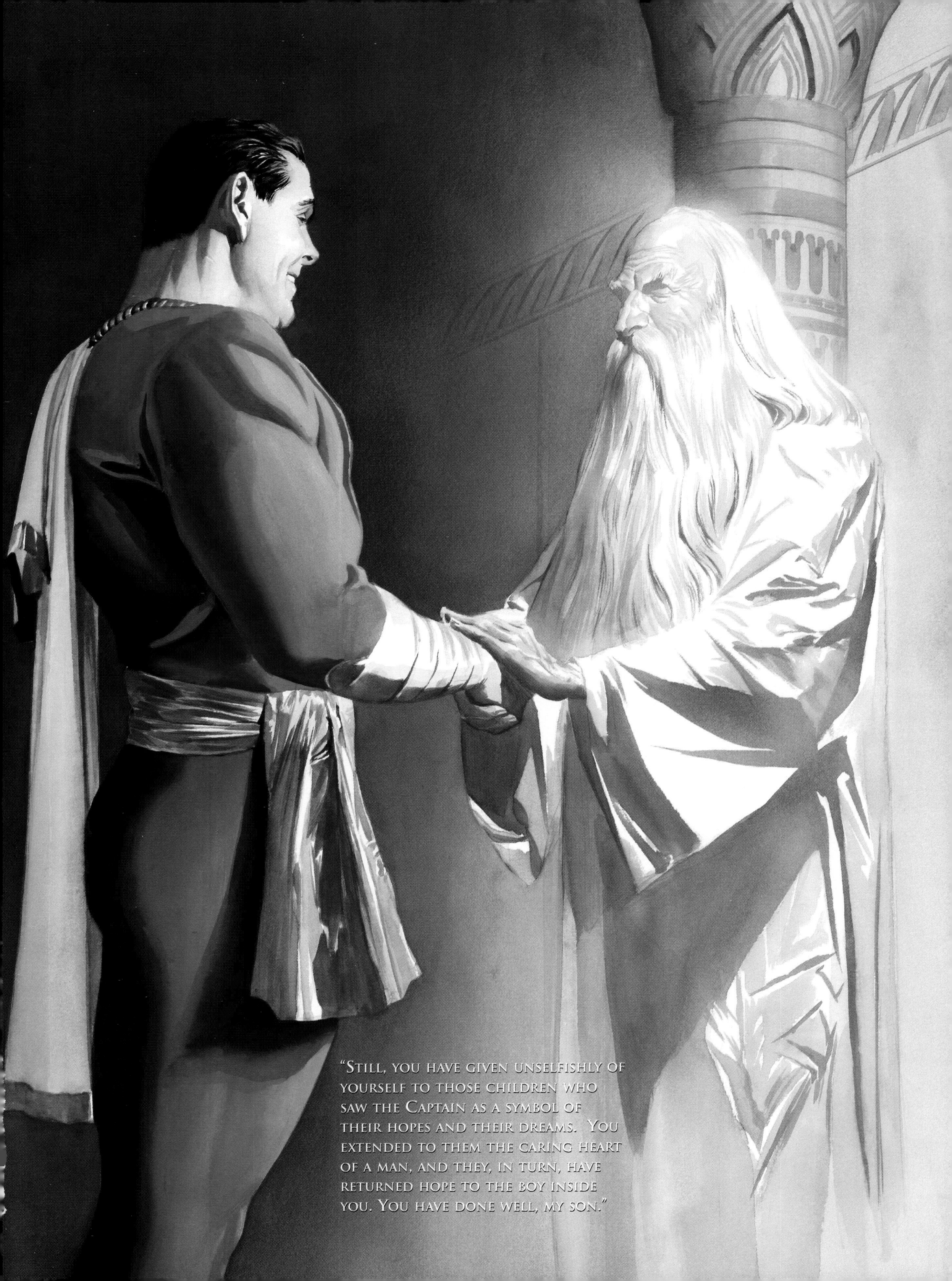
"Still, you have given unselfishly of yourself to those children who saw the Captain as a symbol of their hopes and their dreams. You extended to them the caring heart of a man, and they, in turn, have returned hope to the boy inside you. You have done well, my son."

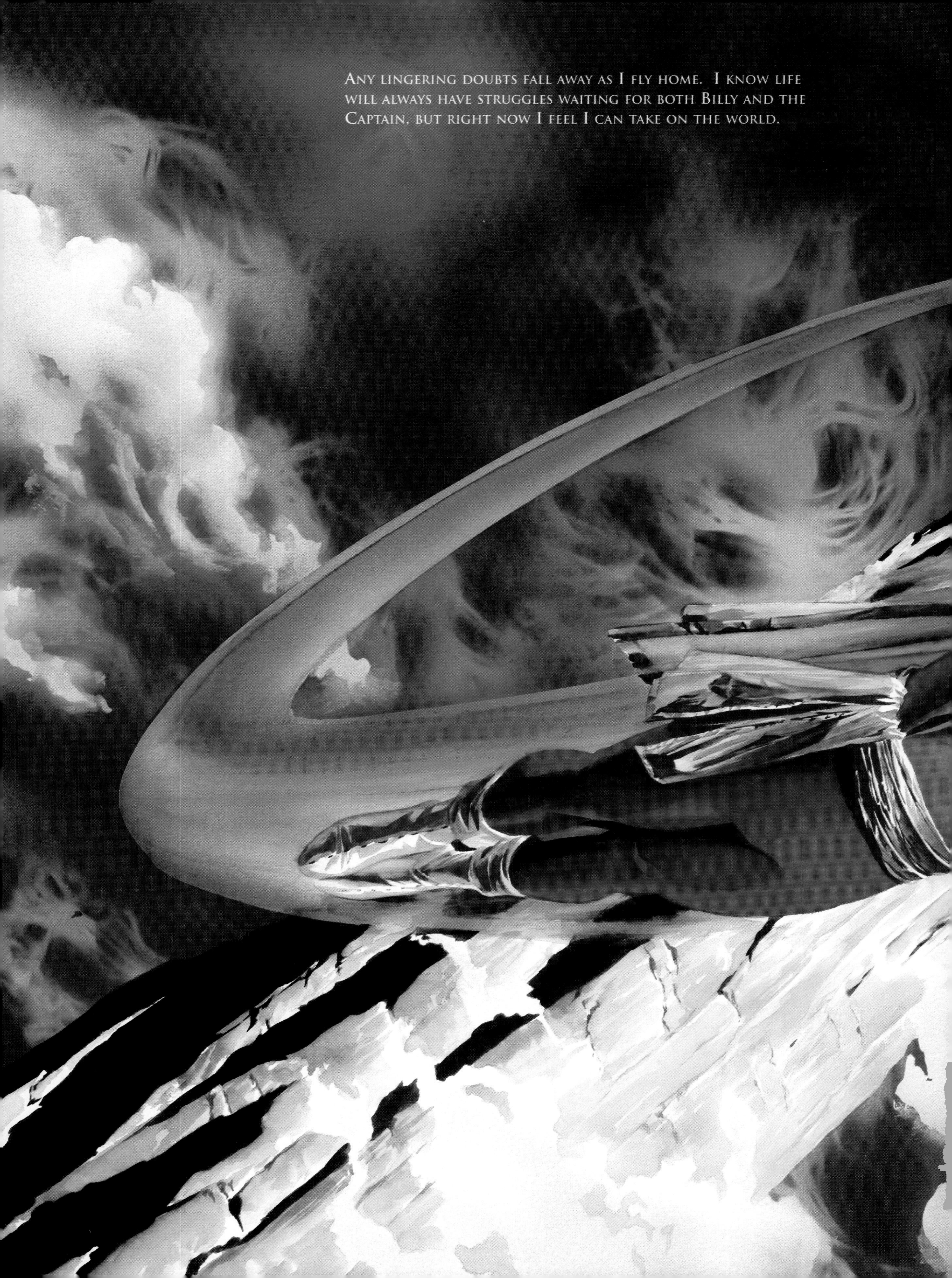
Any lingering doubts fall away as I fly home. I know life will always have struggles waiting for both Billy and the Captain, but right now I feel I can take on the world.

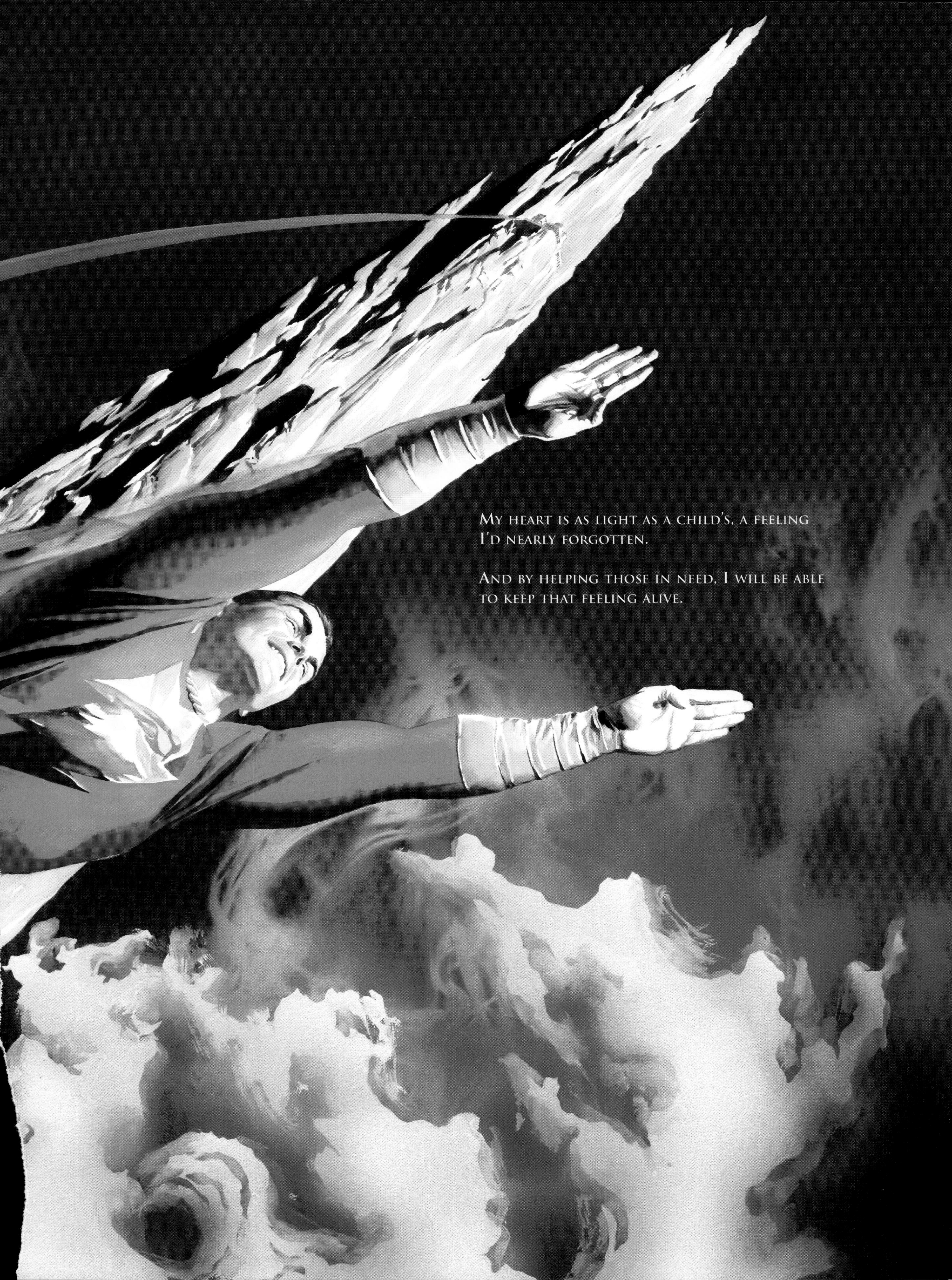
My heart is as light as a child's, a feeling I'd nearly forgotten.
And by helping those in need, I will be able to keep that feeling alive.

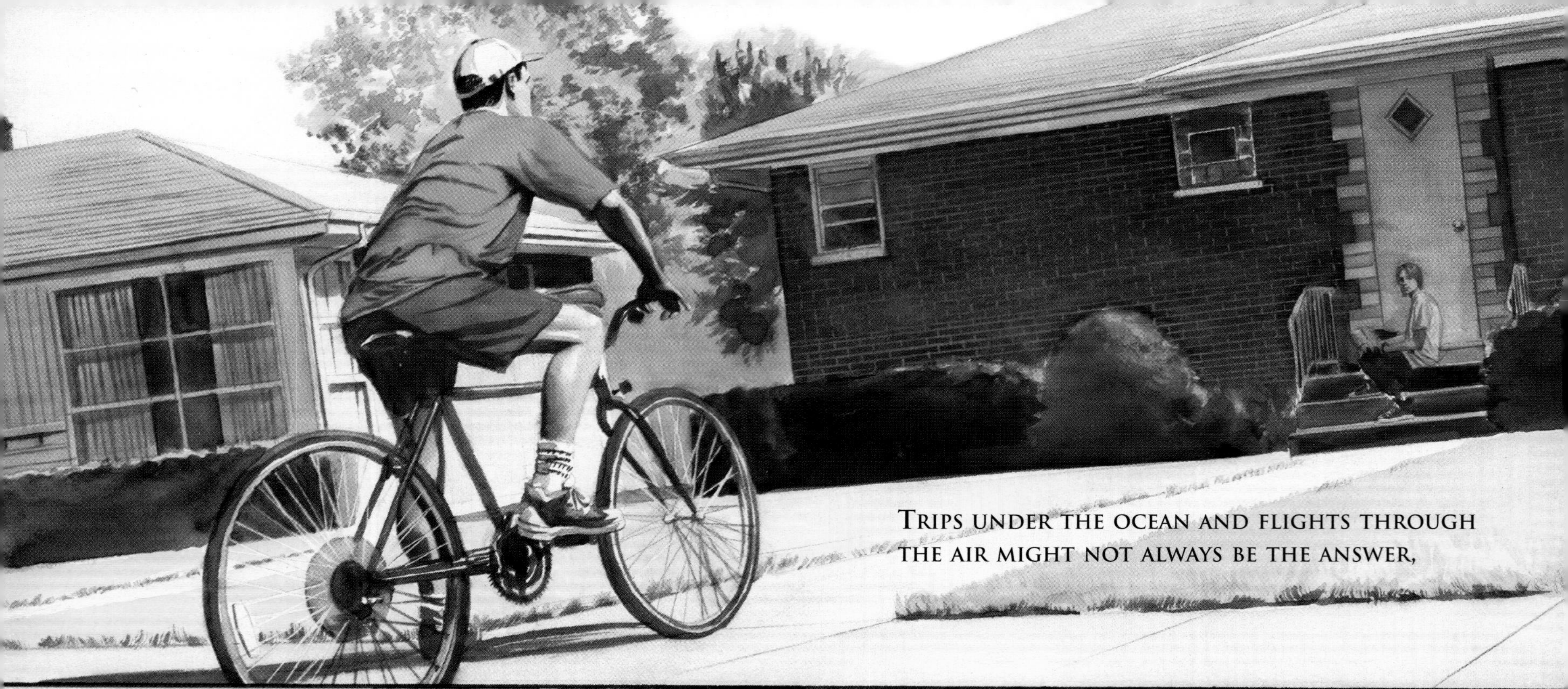
Trips under the ocean and flights through the air might not always be the answer,

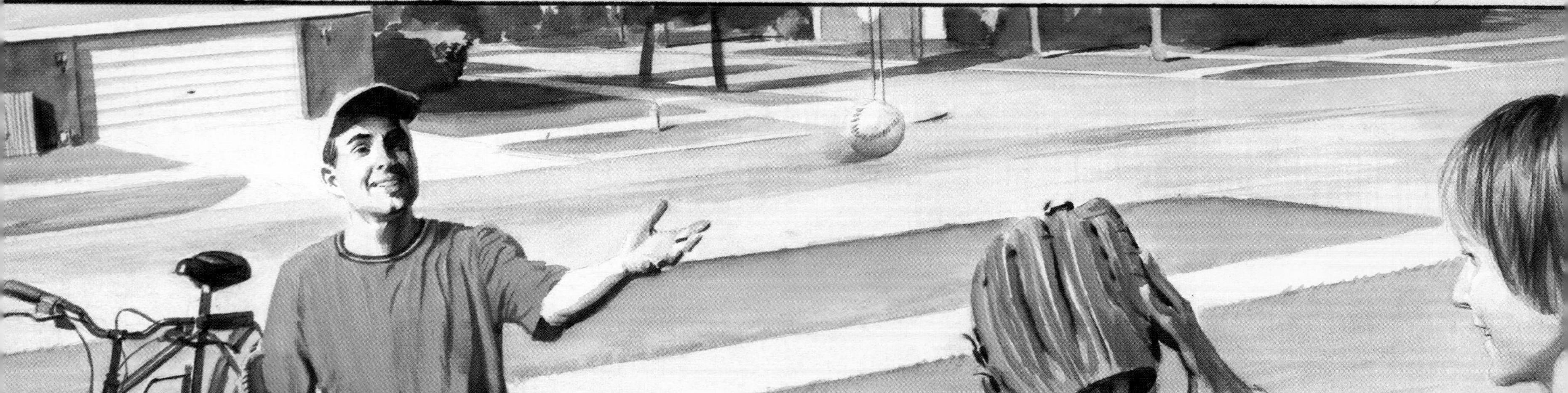
but I can be a friend who will visit when another friend is lonely. I can provide another voice to laugh with.

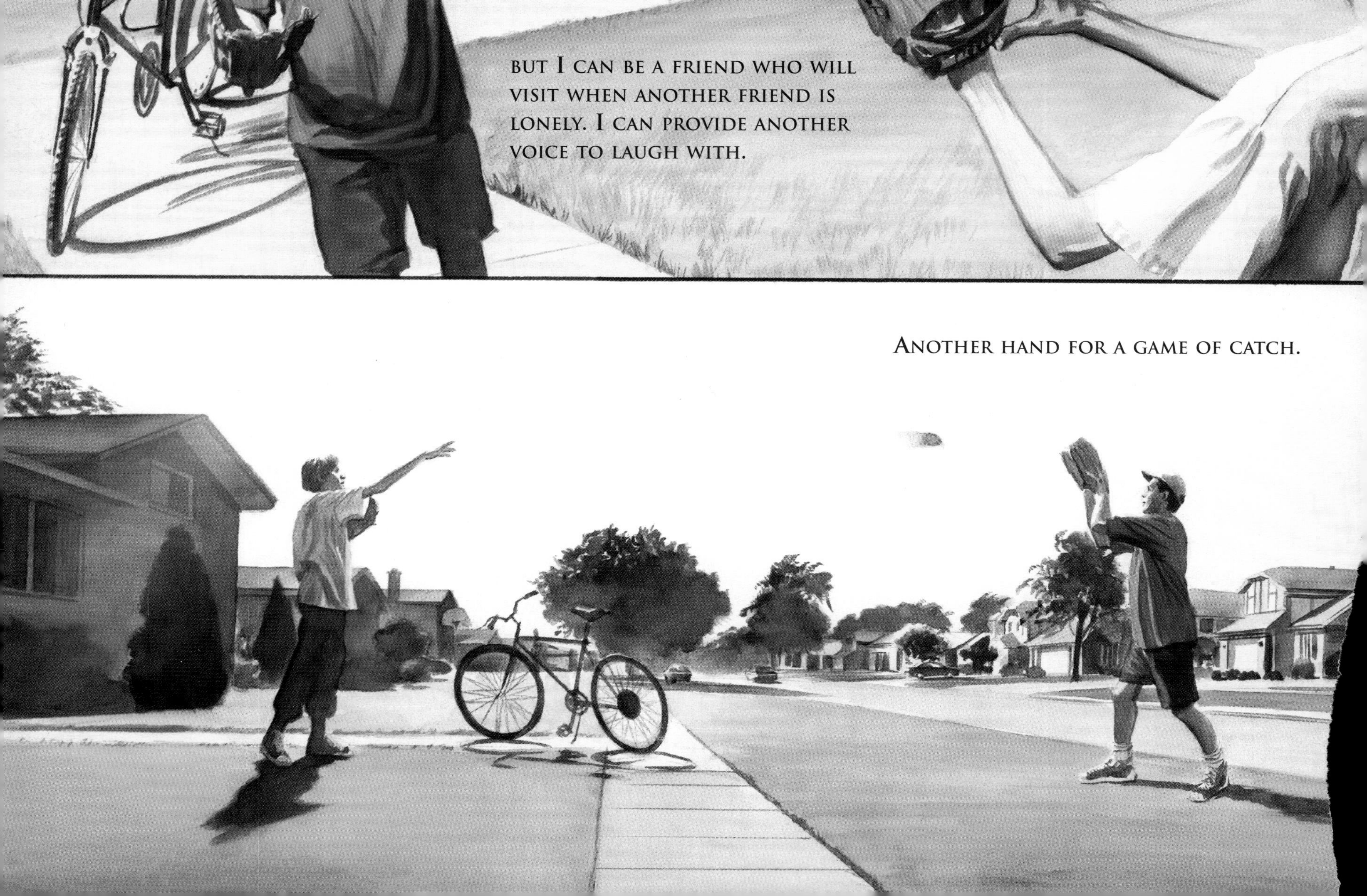
Another hand for a game of catch.